MOM
knows BEST!

MOM
knows BEST!

JOAN WESTER ANDERSON

PLAIN SIGHT PUBLISHING
AN IMPRINT OF CEDAR FORT, INC.
SPRINGVILLE, UTAH

ISBN 13: 978-1-4621-1049-0

Published by Plain Sight Publishing, an imprint of Cedar Fort, Inc.
2373 W. 700 S., Springville, UT, 84663
Distributed by Cedar Fort, Inc., www.cedarfort.com

LIBRARY OF CONGRESS CATALOGING-IN-PUBLICATION DATA

Anderson, Joan Wester, author.
Mom knows best : classic stories every mom will love / Joan Wester Anderson.
pages cm
ISBN 978-1-4621-1049-0
1. Parent and child--Anecdotes. 2. Motherhood--Anecdotes. 3. Anderson, Joan Wester. I. Title.

HQ755.85.A53 2012
306.874'3--dc23

2011049291

Cover design by Angela D. Olsen
Cover design © 2012 by Lyle Mortimer
Edited and typeset by Kelley Konzak

Printed in the United States of America

10 9 8 7 6 5 4 3 2 1

Printed on acid-free paper

To Kelly, Sean, Jack, Michael, and MaryBeth,

my littlest angels.

Introduction

Hi, friends. It's me again. Many of you may already know me if you've read *Moms Go Where Angels Fear to Tread,* a book I wrote describing family life. So many of you asked for a sequel (okay, so my best girlfriend from college and my mother asked for a sequel) that I relented, and did book two, which you are now holding in your hands.

Actually, it was probably a logical progression. *Moms Go Where Angels Fear to Tread* started with the happy newlyweds and went on to describe the early years of family life. There were some stories of teenagers, but, mercifully, not too many. Hopefully the book entertained women of all ages but prepared the younger ones (without necessarily terrorizing them) for what lay ahead.

Book two, therefore, continues the story. At this point, the diapers, strollers, and strained spinach have been put away, although yes, there are a few tales from the earlier trenches just in case you have forgotten how blissful those days really were. This book addresses the inevitable changes in family life, such as dating, proms, jobs, college experiences, and the ever-present text messages. But it also points out the ambivalent nature of parenting during the second half of the job. This is

1

the time when we may be most confused because of the following questions:

- Do we/do we not want our children to grow up, prepare to leave home and put into practice all those theories we've been mouthing at them for the past decade or so? (If the answer is "yes," then why is it so hard for us to *let go*?)
- Will we/won't we manage to stand firm on principles as much for the last child as for the first (although each argument is sapping our aging nerve centers more than the last one did)?
- Are we/aren't we, as couples, still interested in each other as soul-mates and friends? (Midlife divorces are no longer rare, as spouses who have failed to nurture their relationships during these trying times decide to look for something better.)
- During the first half of our journey, we were physically needed. Now it's more about emotions; spiritual and intellectual issues; and how a family survives parental midlife crises, teenaged hormones, and sometimes elder needs at the same time.

It's enough to make us get on the waiting list for that comfy nursing home . . . except there's just one thought being overlooked:

We don't have to know everything on day one. (Say it again.)

If you are a mom with your first two-year-old, ask yourself this question: Were you an expert on icky diapers, ruffles versus knits, or even pet dander on the day your baby was born? Had you ever *thought* about these topics? Of course not. You learned as you went. That was God's plan, and it still is.

Now that you have grade-schoolers, is it your job to worry

about the proper college experience or where you'd like to live when you retire? Why bother? If it's important when you get closer to the time, you'll have the answer. God promised.

(Yes, He did. He gave us an instruction booklet for every job we need to do on this planet—that's the Bible, in case you were wondering—and there are many examples of good parenting included in its pages. Christ himself came to us as a tiny, vulnerable child, and even though his mother and foster father were saints, they still had the problems we do. And I'm sure they didn't make things worse by worrying about things that hadn't occurred yet, and might never.)

A very important thing happens to us at the supermarket, the doctor's office, the committee meeting, and the dinner table, wherever we are in our child-rearing career. We discover that we are up to the challenge. Somehow along the way, perhaps even when we least noticed it, we have learned the art of being flexible, adapting to unexpected happenings, thinking on our feet, waiting it out, and saying "I love you" even when it's hard. As our children have grown, so have we. And coping today is—amazingly—a whole lot easier than we ever thought it would be, when we leaned over the crib and cooed at our future teen.

So here's book two, and I hope it brings you laughter and perhaps a tear or two. Please remember that help is available and love is contagious.

My Resolutions, for Other People

I made a list of New Year's resolutions for everyone," I announced, handing Husband a three-foot length of paper. "These are yours."

He stared at my scribbling. "Sure you haven't forgotten anything?" he asked sarcastically. "Is this all I'm supposed to accomplish this year?"

"Not necessarily. But it'll do for starters."

January, as we all know, is the time to make promises. But through the years I've discovered that the resolutions I make for myself usually don't pan out. There was the year I determined to master in-line skating, the year I resolved to read (and understand) the daily futures, and the decade I attempted to catch up with the ironing and return my library books on time. After all these fiascos, I've decided to make promises for other people instead. It'll be fun seeing how quickly they shape up.

For example, I realized last week that my spouse needs a lot of help in the getting-fit department. "Let's see . . . you signed up for the rec center in January, March, May, and July," I mused, staring at the scrawled appointments on the outgoing calendar. "Did you ever *go?*"

"Never got to it," he admitted. "I'm thinking about just walking around the block instead."

"You signed up for that in September," I pointed out. "That was the same week you enrolled in the Adult Education Heart Healthy class and scheduled three days to dig out those tree stumps in the back. Did you ever *do* any of that?"

"That was also the week they reran the Masters Tournament," he reminded me. "You wouldn't expect me to miss that, would you?"

"Speaking of golf," I remarked in a clever segue, "were you planning to put your clubs away for the winter? They're taking up a lot of space in the laundry room."

"I was thinking about doing that."

"How much longer do you need to think?"

"I'll let you know."

Yes, Husband has a problem with follow-through. But the calendar reveals my weaknesses too. I apparently spent seventy-two hours last year on family dental and doctor appointments, eighty-one hours playing bridge, ninety-seven at choir practice, and an unspeakable amount of time hanging around the service station waiting for my car to be fixed. "If you had used all that time on an outside job," Husband said, "we'd probably be millionaires by now."

"You know I don't want a job that requires wearing shoes."

"Well . . ." he shrugged, "the whole secret of accomplishment is time management. Maybe you should think of that as a New Year's resolution."

"Just as soon as you dig out those stumps," I told him sweetly.

In addition to a new fitness routine, Husband will develop a passing acquaintance with the vacuum cleaner, finish painting the garage (a project started in 2007), and remember to pay the bills.

He'll clean out his closet and throw away his high school letter sweater (the one missing six buttons), and he will abandon Friday night poker games in favor of having "meaningful dialogue" with me. He will refrain from noticing any woman at a party who just earned her doctorate, is a natural blonde, is bilingual, or is on a weight-gaining diet. It's going to be quite a year.

I've got some suggestions for our adolescents too. Sweet Sixteen will discover that she has legs and can actually walk two blocks to the drugstore cosmetic counter for an emergency eyelash curler rather than driving the distance. College Son will perceive that bending over to pick up dirty socks from the bathroom floor qualifies as bodybuilding. This odd couple will also conclude that they prefer Bach to rock, and strains of the New York Philharmonic will waft through the house. They won't panic if it's been two hours since their last shampoos and will insist on cooking gourmet meals for the family on a regular basis (with kitchen cleanup included in the arrangement). Daughter will purge "Oh, Mother-r-r" from her vocabulary and date only boys of whom her father approves (always returning home before ten p.m.) Son will tire of checking the refrigerator at ten-minute intervals and widen his vocabulary beyond "Who, me?" and "Pass the potatoes."

Grade-schoolers will remember to bring home notes, especially those pertaining to maternal field trip chaperone duty and canceled school days, and will make the honor roll every semester. They will develop distaste for refined sugar, stop sleeping with the dog, and call a moratorium on teasing, bickering, sneering, and whining—at least until spring when they can do it outside.

I have a list of resolutions for other people too. The couple down the street who own four Great Danes and rev their motorcycles at dawn will move, to be replaced by an apple-cheeked grandmother who wants children to visit her on rainy days (and

will teach them to bake while their mothers visit the local spa).
The Cub Scout leader will decide she doesn't need my services
as den mother another year and will throw an appreciation ban-
quet for me (no Cub Scouts will be invited.) The orthodontist
will phone apologetically, explaining that someone else's X-rays
got mixed up with our child's (the curse of having a name like
Anderson) and she will not need braces after all. Our supermarket
manager will honor my expired coupons, friends will invite us
to parties only when we are free to attend, peace treaties will be
signed, droughts and floods declared illegal, and all "handyman
special" houses will come equipped with handymen. Families will
schedule a daily prayer time together, and if parents forget, children will remind them.

There will be gas in the car and a Blackberry in every room;
coat zippers won't ever stick, and the paint we just chose for the
master bedroom will perfectly match the bedspread I bought on
sale last fall.

Best of all, the family will keep smiling even when I can't.
"Thanks for the resolutions, Mom," they'll tell me. "You always
know just what to do."

Welcome, New Year. You're going to be wonderful!

A happy New Year! Grant that I
May bring no tear to any eye
When this New Year in time shall end
Let it be said I've played the friend,
Have lived and loved and labored here,
And made of it a happy year.

—Edgar Guest

The Best Years . . . ?

With wisdom born of a sense of hard-earned perspective, I have something to say to the young mothers of America. Yes, you, the lady with the toddler clawing at your leg, a screaming baby balanced precariously over one shoulder, a preschooler about to dash into traffic. You who can spring up the stairs at fifty miles an hour in response to a sudden shriek (or worse, a sudden silence); you who conduct all your adult conversations holding something plastic to your ear, even though the person talking to you is standing right there.

No matter what anyone tells you, these are not the best years of your life.

Yes, I know. Everyone over the age of fifty tells you that you're in your prime. No gray hair, lots of vitality, and, even better, the chance to spend every waking moment with your wee ones. "Enjoy them while they're young," the older generation advises, misty-eyed. "At least you know where they are at night. Little people, little problems. Time passes all too quickly . . ." Yada, yada. Then these tenderhearted souls skip off to a bridge club luncheon, a satisfying part-time job or volunteer position, a round of golf—and return to a spotless house unsullied by crushed cracker crumbs underfoot or muddy handprints on the new "dry clean only" comforter.

In one way, the older generation is quite right. There is probably no time more *critical* than those first formative years of childhood. It is now that the seeds of self-discipline, respect, sociability, and lots of other emotional imperatives are sown and nurtured. How a child is treated and trained as a preschooler can have an enormous bearing on what kind of adult he someday becomes. A maxim of the Jesuits couldn't be more accurate: "Give us the boy until he is seven, and we will give you the man."

However, those who are far removed from daily diaper duty sometimes regard the *importance* of early childhood as synonymous with *enjoyment* of such. This is a mistake. I've no doubt that Mr. Two-Year-Old enjoys his life quite a bit, but I know very few mothers of two-year-olds who giggle their way through each fun-filled moment. Most of them are quietly counting the days until preschool while also feeling guilty that they don't seem to be enjoying "the best years of your life."

Well, they aren't the best years. Face it—what's "best" about

- being in a crowded elevator and having Mr. Four ask you in his most piercing voice, "Mommy, why were you and Daddy yelling this morning? Huh, Mommy? Huh?"
- trying to spend just three minutes alone in the bathroom. And regarding this achievement as the high point of your day.
- having your tot fill her pants just as the pediatrician's nurse announces, "You may come in now, Mrs. Anderson."
- discovering that your three-year-old has knocked over a display of beach balls at the Dollar Store. Actually, the whole store has discovered it, and everyone is looking at you.

To be honest, some mothers do enjoy the small-fry stage (these are the same people who like to clean cabinets and wax their driveways.) But most of us just aren't equipped to handle this age group on a continuing basis. Face it—did anything in your "Great Philosophies of the Orient" class prepare you for the toddler who asks "Why?" at five-minute intervals during the day? Did your years as a CPA lay any groundwork for handling the tot who's been screaming since noon because he left his beloved plush bunny at the store (and you can't remember if it was the farmer's market or the dollar store)? No, the problem lies not in our confusion over the preschool set but in the fact that they come into our lives *first*, and what do we have to compare their stages with?

As one battle-scarred veteran, I advise you to forget your dreams of sanity and organization. Instead, some adjustments in your thoughts and behavior will make these days more bearable.

Learn to run. If you're already a tennis star or champion sprinter, so much the better. But most of us move through life at a more sedate pace, broken only by an occasional dash for the train or a wild clean-the-apartment-in-ten-minutes-before-the-in-laws-arrive binge. Motherhood, however, demands a level of fitness that few of us have ever attained. Is the nine-month-old teetering precariously on the top step? Has Miss Two decided to chase Daddy's car—down the middle of the street? Is the toddler reaching determinedly for the aspirin bottle on the highest shelf? "You go, girl!" can't begin to cover our response, but the three-minute mile will definitely do.

Get used to crumbs. From the time you begin raising your brood, crumbs will be your constant companions—on top of, next to, or underneath any place you are. You will find them snuggled in your dresser drawers, embedded in your hairbrush, on the front seat of your car, inside your purse. No one understands the "how" or "why" of it, but wherever little ones gather, crumbs seem sure to follow. It's no use buying a better broom or even running home to Mother. Instead, simply accept the presence of these uninvited boarders, and perhaps you'll get used to them someday.

Forget about answering questions that start with "Why?," "How come?," "What?," and "Where?" Yes, I know. A parent is a child's first and most important teacher, and you do take your responsibilities seriously. But it's estimated that a young child asks about fifty questions per day (it seems like much more), so if you multiply that by the number of small fries in your domain, and then try to answer every query in a truthful and professional manner . . . well, it hardly leaves time for those romance novels, does it?

On the other hand, no parent wants to appear disinterested where her offspring are concerned. So the best solution after "Go look it up on Wikipedia" is to always answer a question of *theirs* with a question of *yours*. You'll be surprised where this can lead.

("What would happen if I flushed clay down the toilet, Mommy?"

"What do *you* think, sweetheart?"

"I think you better come and look.")

Do not become too attached to material possessions. Peanut butter on ceiling-to-floor drapes can be cleaned away and, after a clever retouching, no one will notice those child-made scratches on the dining room table. But if you discover one morning that your second grader has been dropping your Civil War coin collection into vending machines all summer, it could be the beginning of cardiac arrest.

Instead, put aside thoughts of white carpet until the kids

are in grad school and spend your extra money on memories. A video camcorder, scrapbooks, special days at the zoo, or family reunions—how much more rewarding than possessions that wither or fade?

Don't try to decide what you do all day. I know what my husband *thinks* I do all day. During the morning hours, I watch *Oprah* reruns or *Dr. Phil* while putting lint on his black socks. While sipping an afternoon lemonade, I give all his tools to the children with instructions to distribute them in other people's garages.

Once, when the kids were tiny, I decided to show him what I do each day by simply not doing it. When he left for work, I gathered an armload of magazines, locked away all dangerous substances, and stretched out on the couch. Though it took our preschoolers several stunned moments to realize that today the usual rules did not apply, they soon got into the spirit of the thing. They turned their mattresses into trampolines, scattered the contents of several cereal boxes throughout the apartment, artistically trailed toilet paper from the light fixtures, crayoned the walls, and tap-danced on the kitchen counters. My contribution was to make no contribution, aside from washing small hands, faces, and bottoms and cheering their escapades. When one meal or snack ended, I simply shoved the sticky dishes across the table to make room for the next, and we left the wet diapers wherever they fell.

By six p.m., the children were exhausted, and the apartment looked as if a hurricane had swept through. When my husband came in, he slipped on an apple core and stood in shocked silence surveying the wreckage.

"You asked me what I do all day," I spoke sweetly from the couch. "Well, now you know. I keep all this from happening."

Husband didn't speak to me for at least an hour. But he did help to clean up the mess (it took three days) and never asked that question again.

Mothering brings different rewards at different ages, and if you're less than thrilled about the beginning of the journey, stick around. Perhaps your enjoyment factor is going to zoom upward when your child gets to be six or even sixteen. You may find that you were born to be a Girl Scout leader and absolutely enjoy teenagers, even your own. (Yes, it can happen, and I have a houseful to prove it!)

In the meantime, cuddle your little ones, play with them, sing songs, go for nature walks, kiss "owies," collect hugs, take advantage of all grandparent babysitting offers, thank God for the marvel of His creations. And be patient—the best years of *your* life may be just around the corner.

Wondering Where
They Came From

O*ne of* the advantages of having a fairly large family is that each member brings a unique perspective to the group-at-large. (Sometimes, during desperate moments, that seems to be the *only* advantage.) One can assume that husband and wife share at least some similar interests and viewpoints; otherwise, why would they have gotten married? But as offspring arrive, the scenario is apt to shift. The couple who loathe sports, for instance, may have to deal with an eight-year-old who eats, dreams, and breathes Little League. The mother who has two left feet may be presented with a budding ballerina. A permissive pair may produce a Judge Judy—it's testimony to the Lord's sense of humor that He so often mixes diverse personalities within the same household. But as my children grow, I can also see the blessings in such a system. If all the kids in a family were alike, all simply clones of dear old Mom and Dad, what a wealth of new experiences we'd be missing!

My husband and I once lunched with a friend who is an electrical engineer. We made the mistake of asking him what his job entailed, and for the next half hour, he spoke in tongues, or at least it seemed so to us. Spouse and I both struggled with math in school (Spouse still can't understand a valid *reason* for math after long division) and crept lightly through our minimum science requirements, hoping not to be noticed. Yet God has seen fit to grace us with a son who began assembling miniature skeleton bones from the time he was a toddler, owned a high-powered microscope (complete with bug slides) during middle school, and now regards the Fundamental Theorem of Differ-Integral Calculus one of the bright spots in his life.

For many years, as I bought chemistry sets or books involving PI as Christmas presents, I assumed that there had been a mix-up in the maternity ward and I would one day find my real child, probably in a remedial biology class. But now that I see the folly of my thinking, Son not only looks vaguely like our cousins from Belgium, Wisconsin, but can also fix circuit breakers and calculate how many tiles we should buy to cover the roof, just like his grandfather can. I don't know what gene combination produced him, but I'm certainly counting my blessings.

Then there's the child who pleaded for flute lessons in fourth grade. "I don't know one end of a flute from the other," I protested. "I won't be able to help you at all."

Did Son look relieved? "I promise I'll practice in the garage," he begged. "I'll walk the cat every night, I'll clean out the dirty socks under my bed, I'll even eat boiled cabbage without grabbing my throat and falling to the floor . . ."

"Enough. Where do I sign?"

Little did I know then that Son and flute would open a new world for the rest of the family. Band concerts. The 1812 Overture. Solo contests. A twenty-piece marching uniform. ("Have you got your spats? Gauntlet? Plume?") Competition at Disney World. Memorial Day parades. And of course a learning experience for Mom. "Your arpeggios have improved, honey." I gave him my professional opinion after the last performance. "But you still need a little work on that staccato passage." (And I wouldn't have missed a note of it.)

Daughter, contrary to expectations, has not introduced us to a life of dancing class, frills, and Barbie dolls, but her family contribution is still valuable. How else would I have become acquainted with the finer points of soccer (and the fun of screaming at a referee) than through her Saturday afternoon games? Flushed, bleeding from a cut lip, cleats clanking, she barely resembles the ruffled and ribboned toddler she once was (when I controlled her closet). And during quieter moments, she shares her other hobby—video games—with a bemused Daddy, who still can't top her highest score. An unexpected personality, but I wouldn't care to swap the real person for the image.

Enjoying new experiences, compliments of one's children, can be broadening, provided one does not invest heavily in equipment, lessons, or uniforms for at least a year to see if the thrill will last. I well remember Third Son's bodybuilding period, which involved a cumbersome set of weights, Tuesday evening chauffeur duty for judo class, and liver-and-spinach menus—lasting a scant four months. Son did develop some impressive biceps, and I found a new glue for mending split chairs, but we had to host a garage sale to clear out the equipment and how-to books. It wasn't a week later that this same boy entered his debating phase, plunging into research, practicing arguments at the dinner table, and sporting an official-looking briefcase to team events. This period lasted long enough for him to collect a few trophies, but his logic skills left their mark on us.

"You may either a) paint the porch, b) hire a painter, or c) accept a citation from the building inspector," I told Husband recently.

"Objection," Husband retorted smoothly. "That statement is irrelevant, immaterial, and . . ."

"Point of order, Mr. Chairman," I interspersed. "Counsel wishes to state . . ."

Whatever the outcome, it's interesting to utilize techniques learned from our offspring. In fact, our whole existence is enlivened, deepened, and enriched by the contributions they make to family life.

Thank you, God, for children, especially when they don't resemble their parents at all.

Children in a family are like flowers in a bouquet: there's always one determined to face in an opposite direction from the way the arranger desires.

—*Marcelene Cox*

Love Thy Neighbor

You'll remember from *Moms Go Where Angels Fear to Tread* that when we bought our Handyman Special home on Hickory Avenue, we thought we were purchasing bigger rooms, a fourth bedroom, an extra bath, a large weeping willow tree, and a garage in which to store Husband's modest screwdriver collection. We didn't know then that we were also buying a neighborhood. Or that it would turn out to be the most blessed purchase we ever made.

I should have guessed that the area was tailor-made for our children when we pulled up on moving day to find eight small boys lounging on our lawn. "We came to welcome you to the neighborhood and see if you want to buy any blueberries," explained one child, who looked as if his face had been dipped in blue ink.

"Or band concert tickets," said another, holding an ominous-looking trombone.

"Or maybe a puppy?" a third suggested hopefully. "We've got *lots* of them at our house."

"Sorry," I told them. "We owe our next three paychecks to the moving company. But it was nice of you to drop by. Do you all live near here?"

Husband, who had been staring nervously at an immense pile of bicycles in our driveway, grabbed my arm as the kids pointed. "You don't mean," he croaked, "that you all live in the houses next door?"

They nodded. "Of course," said Blue Boy, "our older brothers are at work."

"And the little guys are napping," Trombone pointed out.

Sometime during the next year, when we had recovered sufficiently to take an accurate tally, we determined that our cluster of five homes contained a total of eighteen sons. Our daughter's birth the following summer brought the female population to a pathetic four. So many male children seemed ecologically unsound and perhaps even slightly un-American. But by that time we had already begun to enjoy the benefits.

Since all of the boys traveled in a pack (somewhat resembling a formation of locusts) from tree fort to sandbox to backyard baseball diamond, it became almost impossible to discover at a glance which blue-jeaned lad was responsible for a particular bit of mayhem. I may have had a sneaking suspicion that Charlie draped our evergreens with bathroom tissue. But how could I speak to his mother, Mary Alice, about it when it was a foregone conclusion that one of *my* sons, in training for the US Open, would eventually whack off the heads of her petunias with his five iron?

Instead, we mothers shared a tacit agreement—if the crime was minor, we all looked the other way or retreated to the kitchen to peel parsley until our nerves had stopped quivering. If the deed was of major importance, however, heavy artillery was called in, in the form of five fathers who sentenced everyone, innocent or guilty, to a term of hard labor cleaning basements.

On summer Sundays, more often than not, we'd gather in

the late afternoon in one or two connecting yards, bringing play-
pens, grills, and hot dogs. These gatherings started as a welcome
opportunity for adults to enjoy eye-level conversations, but we
soon discovered that the child-benefits were unlimited. A teen-
age daughter whose sole comment all summer had been an exas-
perated, "Oh, Mother-r-r-r" found that she could easily unburden
herself to someone else's Mother-r-r-r without fear of reprisal
or embarrassment. The third-grader whose unreasonable dad
refused to let him set off firecrackers in the church parking lot
discovered that someone else's dad was also adamant on the subject. The gatherings, according to ground rules, always included
at least one argument about the state of the union, the state of the
parish, or the state of a particular child's bedroom. But everyone's
opinion was valued and accepted, especially if delivered while
standing dramatically on top of a picnic table. (Which explains
why many of our kids are now planning careers in law or politics).

Neither we nor our neighbors thought of moving away when
household space became a premium. Unless getting transferred,
most families decided to build additions rather than pack up.
And several actually moved up or down the street, as their needs
changed. Our family put "dibs" on at least two houses through the
years but were outbid when the time actually came.

Since we were sharing each other's children, it became only
natural to share each other's belongings as well, starting, I suppose, on the day my husband found a note in the garage where
the plunger had been hanging. "No time to ask—just TOOK!" a
frantic Bob had scrawled.

"Poor guy," Spouse sighed. "I suppose his two-year-old was
flushing apples down the toilet again."

"I think it's more serious than that," I mused, staring out the
window at the truck marked Flood Control. "One of Bob's kids is

carrying a canoe *into* the kitchen."

That's when we decided to offer equipment on a round-the-clock basis, realizing that someone developing an urgent midnight need for a flashlight can't waste time searching for one under a stack of laundry. Likewise, anyone simultaneously saddled with chicken pox and a sick puppy needed all the moral support (and upholstery shampoo) she can get. And if a neighbor was in trouble, people also lent themselves. One Christmas Eve, Bob (of canoe fame) spent hours in our crawl space thawing frozen pipes with his daughter's hair drier. His way of saying "thanks" for the just-in-time plunger.

The years have slid by quickly, one against the other, since that memorable moving day. Our "bigger rooms and extra bath" have shrunk to amazingly small proportions, while Husband's screwdriver collection now takes up the entire garage. The faces at our summer gatherings have changed too; one boy has left to become a priest, others have married, and three preschool ballerinas have evened the male/female ratio just a bit.

But these are only surface changes, like the subtle maturing of a beloved child. What is really critical, and continues to be, is the care and concern our neighbors give to one another. In sharing sandboxes, gray hair, and fuses, we've discovered we're also sharing our hearts.

Count your life by smiles, not tears.
Count your age by friends, not years

—*Unknown*

In Front of a Roaring Fire

*B*ut *what* do you people *do* up here during the winter?" asked my new neighbor, bravely resisting the impulse to burst into tears. We were shivering together in front of her house into which her family had transferred from (sigh) Florida only two weeks earlier, and she was having some minor difficulties adjusting to the Midwest ambiance—subzero winds, barren landscapes, and frozen water pipes.

"Do?" I resisted a smug you-think-this-is-bad-you-should-have-seen-the-winter-of-'07 answer and opted instead for helpful honesty. "Well, we start projects."

"Projects?"

"Uh-huh. We learn how to carve bookends or take a course in French cooking or French itself, or we decide to read every Agatha Christie mystery before Groundhog Day . . ."

"Gee." There was a tentative touch of hope in her eyes. "Imagine, hooking a rug in front of a roaring fire . . ."

"We have central heating here in Illinois," I informed her.

". . . Or spinning your own cloth or dipping candles . . ."

"Actually," I said, clearing my throat, "most of us don't go quite that far. A semester or two of Swim and Trim . . ."

"Oh, I think it's a wonderful idea!" she enthused. "It'll never surpass surfing by moonlight, but at least it passes the time, doesn't it?"

"Now you're getting the idea," I told her and then hacked my way home through the ice floes.

My own winter projects were already in full swing in the den. I was finishing a needlepoint wall hanging begun in 2006 to complement our green-and-gold living room. However, our living room was now blue, the yarn shop had gone out of business, and I had always hated needlepointing. My exercise chart was hung neatly on the door, hand-lettered during last month's subzero stretch, outlining my fitness program. I hadn't started yet, since exercise makes me hungry, but the chart, everyone agreed, was a real eye-catcher.

Then there was my pile of correspondence, both e- and snail-mail, mostly dating back to the summer I had surgery. All those encouraging notes and get-well cards certainly deserved a hand-written response, and I had saved them for a slack time when I could give them the attention they deserved. It was true that by now few included return addresses (I had forgotten to save the envelopes) and were simply signed "Stacie" or "Barbara" (Would that be my aunt Barbara in Cleveland or Barbara my classmate from high school or Barbara from the church Woman's Club?), but one of these days I fully intended to start on that stack. Husband had remarked only yesterday that it was becoming a fire hazard.

Winter dragged on, and the first crocuses were actually struggling through the drifts before I met my new neighbor again. "Welcome to spring!" I told her as we slogged together through the supermarket parking lot.

"Huh?" She looked up at the overcast sky. "When is it coming?"

"We had spring last Sunday," I told her. "You were probably still hibernating."

"Oh, right. We took the kids to a movie and missed the whole thing. No wonder the neighbors were out pointing to the sky when we returned. And all those TV news cameras . . ."

"There's always next year," I assured her. "How did winter go? Did you start any projects?"

"Did I!" She grinned. "I grew my fingernails, learned several Russian verbs, and collected feathers."

"I'm impressed," I told her sincerely.

"There was just one problem," she began hesitantly.

"What?"

"I never *finished* anything."

I patted her shoulder. "Now you've got the whole idea."

"Well . . ." She sighed. "It'll never replace picking oranges in February, but at least we survived."

I think she's going to fit in well.

Winter, a lingering season, is a time to gather golden moments, embark upon a sentimental journey, and enjoy every idle hour.

—John Boswell

Different Strokes

• •

Recently I witnessed a debate between parents on why boys and girls behave differently. One group felt that it was all the result of early conditioning; we programmed little boys to bash each other with toy trucks and gave dolls to little girls—hence, males grew up to be aggressive, and females, nurturers. The second group felt that the differences were DNA-inspired, and no amount of training could alter such basic behavior.

I don't know the answer (if there even is one), but as a mother of both genders (and a confirmed kid-watcher), I can testify that from the earliest stages in life, boys and girls do view the world differently. And seeing life through the eyes of one sex versus the other becomes an interesting study in contrasts for parents too.

Here, then, are some random musings on boy-girl behavior. See how closely your impressions match mine:

If you put a pink ribbon in your baby boy's hair (only in the privacy of your own home, after your husband has left for work, just to see what Junior would have looked like as a girl), Baby Boy will promptly pull it off and eat it. The same ribbon in a baby girl's hair will cause her to crawl to the full-length mirror, preen a bit, and then eat it.

Both sexes seem to enjoy crushing strained spinach gobs

between their fists and rubbing the mess into their ears. But girls will say, "Icky!" while so engaged.

As everyone knows, boys are harder to potty train. So why did my neighbor's daughter carry along a box of disposable diapers to preschool this year? (At least it wasn't first grade.)

Oldest children in a family (whether male or female) tend to be more reliable, trustworthy, and serious than their younger siblings, according to the experts. (My neighbor's damp daughter *is* the oldest. Her carefree younger brother is already trained.)

If you become involved in Scouting and teach a group of Brownies to bake cookies, they will eat half of them. Cub Scouts, by contrast, will set fire to your oven. While on a campout, Cubs will wear the same underwear for three days. Brownies will lose their underwear.

Around the age of eight or nine, little boys will suddenly refuse to play with little girls. Girls, however, don't seem to get the "go away" message for a year or two and will insist they be included in the softball game. Finally, they wash their hands of the whole affair and join a girls' league, at which point boys become interested again and sneak in to watch all the games.

Fifth-grade girls' sleepovers are characterized by night-long giggles and vast quantities of pizza. Wise parents do not host sleepovers for fifth-grade boys unless the crowd will be sleeping in tents at least forty yards from the house, and all forms of weaponry have been confiscated.

Although you have explained the purpose of soap, water, and shampoo to your son since the day of his birth, the message has fallen on deaf ears until he turns eleven or twelve. At which point, he suddenly cannot pass a bathroom without stopping in to take a shower. Your daughter has been carrying a comb around with her since toddler days, when she discovered the purpose of pockets and purses. At eleven or twelve, she suddenly demands pierced ears, four-inch heels, and purple lipstick. (A word of warning: Fathers are especially vulnerable during this stage of their daughters' development. Protect your husband's blood pressure by assuring him that your daughter is thinking about joining a cloistered convent and simply wants to have one last fling.)

High school seems to herald the days of real equality: identical jeans, unisex band uniforms, advanced science for girls, typing class for boys—and boys finally catching up to girls on height charts. However, some differences still remain. Boys, always noted for being direct and outspoken, turn sullen. "Who, me?" is about as chummy as they get. Girls, at least for a while, unleash a veritable flood of small talk, describing clothes, teen conversations, and dating problems in endless detail. Which causes mothers to develop a glassy-eyed stare and utilize ear plugs whenever possible.

Girls develop courteous driving habits, at least when their parents are watching; they signal when making a left turn, stop at railroad crossings (especially when the gates are down) and regard cars as a fun means of transportation. Boys, however, are usually intrigued by peering at carburetors, enjoy honking horns and squealing tires, and regard cars as an extension of their egos. (Note: Fathers are especially vulnerable during this stage of their sons' development. Soothe your husband's ulcer by assuring him that Junior needs to learn how to drive so he can become a foreign missionary in a mountainous jungle.)

At grade-school graduation, girls throw their mortarboards into the air. Boys throw theirs at each other. Either way, parents end up paying for a replacement mortarboard.

I guess we'll never solve the mystery of why the genders are different. But as I watch my kids mature, I can only conclude that none of it really matters. What does matter is the humor, interest, and absolute enjoyment that the kids contribute to the family, each in her or his way.

Viva la difference!

O God, we give you thanks for our children whom you have welcomed into this family. Bless this family. Confirm a lively sense of your presence with us and grant that our lives may show forth the love of Christ, as we bring up our children to love all that is good.

—Prayer for the Beginning of Life,

NCCB, USCC, 1989

How It All Began . . .

As you know, our family had stumbled upon projects as a way to avoid the winter blues several years ago when the kids were little. It started on one of those icy and overcast days when I could no longer bear to enter a particular room in the family abode. The sight of faded walls, drab curtains, and an overall film of neglect was even depressing the dog. Clearly something had to be done.

"What are we going to do about the orange bedroom?" I asked my husband one morning.

Spouse nervously folded the newspaper. "What did you have in mind?"

"Either painting or moving to a new neighborhood."

"Fine, fine," he murmured, reaching around me to grab his car keys. "I'll get right on it."

Three weeks later, on a Sunday afternoon, I broached the subject again, somewhat more firmly. "The orange bedroom needs painting."

"Who threw that pass?" Spouse yelled at the TV sportscaster.

"I have here," I continued calmly, "a bucket of paint and a roller—"

"You can't just paint!" My better half interrupted in alarm.

"The room has to be washed down, spackled, sanded, primed . . . they don't show you any of *those* steps on the Do It Yourself Network, do they?"

"Well?"

"I'll get right on it."

The trouble is, my husband is a meticulous worker. When he has finished painting a room, the entire staff at Home and Garden magazine bows in reverence. His tool collection rivals any hardware store inventory. His repairs—no doubt about it—will last right through the Second Coming. But he has one small flaw that dulls the luster of his accomplishment. He seldom gets right on it.

When three more weeks elapsed, I turned to the children for help and found a willing work force. There is nothing more exciting to school-age boys than the prospect of ripping apart a room and bashing each other with paint brushes. The orange bedroom was inhabited by Second and Third sons (and a host of other living things that I'd rather not mention). In danger of finding a place in the Guinness Book of World Records under "most neglected . . ." the room had not been touched since we moved in and begged for a facelift. We collected our materials, decided on a work motto ("No One Will Ever Notice") and assigned jobs. It was simply a coincidence that Spouse was scheduled to attend a late meeting that evening.

Youngest Son was in charge of Toddler Daughter, keeping her downstairs, amused, and alive at all times. Third Son and I would wash walls while One and Two moved all furniture and debris to a safe location (hopefully, the incinerator). One and Two would then scrub the floor while I broiled some hamburgers, monitored Toddler's activities, and broke up wrestling matches between One, Two, Three, and Four. While floors and walls dried, dinner would be inhaled, Toddler bedded down, and dishes done. The boys and I would then return to the bedroom, ready to paint.

Since Number Two possesses a quirky habit (probably inherited from his neatnik father) of using rulers to judge distance and mixing paint with one of those cute little flat sticks instead of just jiggling the can (my method), he was assigned to detail work. Oldest Boy, in training for junior varsity basketball, would paint ceilings, one leap at a time, and Three was in charge of keeping our rock CDs at highest volume throughout the evening.

Actually, the painting progressed rather well. Although the walls resembled dart boards, Second Son had done an admirable job of patching, and Three had thoughtfully removed his football posters so we wouldn't be tempted to paint around them.

Our first mishap occurred when Daughter, escaping from her crib, toddled in to join the fun and plopped down in the roller pan. She was assured that her help was not needed, but the incident put me in a nostalgic mood. "I remember that February, while we still lived in the apartment, when all you guys had chickenpox," I told them, wiping up spills. "I painted and wallpapered a room in one day and gave you seventeen baking soda baths too."

"I don't remember that," said Four, painting his name on his arm.

"You were too little," Two pointed out, "but I remember. That was the night Dad asked why dinner was late and Mom walked over to Grandma's."

"In a blizzard," added Oldest Son. Ah, memories.

We were almost half-done when the phone rang. In their mad dash to answer what turned out to be a wrong number, two sons bounced off a wet wall and careened into a third, who was at that moment touching up the trim around the wallpaper border.

Fortunately, the damage was nominal and offered us an opportunity to quote our work motto ("No One Will Ever Notice") once more. I quoted a few other phrases as well, but no one paid any attention.

As we finished the last wall, a car turned into the driveway. "It's Dad!" exclaimed Youngest. "Boy, is he gonna be surprised!"

And he was, too. His gaze went from polite to stunned to shocked to aghast to upset and back to polite. We stood at attention, awaiting the verdict.

"If you consider," I finally broke the silence, "that the lamps will divert light *away* from the walls . . ."

"Don't forget," Number One mentioned helpfully, "that the rugs will cover most of those paint blobs on the floor . . ."

"My football posters aren't even up yet," Three volunteered.

"Hmmm," said Spouse.

Later he would remind me that if I'd only curbed my impatience, he could have eventually turned that upstairs stable into a shrine. I know I'm impatient. But really, I'm only thinking of him. Why should he waste his energy on a bedroom when I've already ordered lumber for our new deck?

Dad's Household Handyman Advice

1. Try to work alone. An audience is rarely any help.
2. If what you've done is stupid, but it works, redefine *stupid*.
3. If it's electronic, get a new one ... or consult a twelve-year-old.
4. Keep it simple. Get a new battery, replace the bulb or fuse, see if the tank is empty, try turning the switch on, or just paint over it.

Only Forty-Seven Cents

While we're on the subject of getting organized, spring is also the time when the litter of a household reaches avalanche proportions. Games from Christmas have lost their appeal and languish amid underbed dust in the upstairs landfills. Closets bulge with electronic components, toddler-sized orange raincoats, and bric-a-brac too nice to throw out. "I can't imagine anyone buying this house in its present condition," I murmured one morning.

"Since when are we selling?" Husband looked alarmed. "We're still raising kids, and I'm not ready for a pension yet."

"The children will eventually leave," I replied hopefully. "There's no harm in planning ahead, is there? We could replace the high schooler's Mickey Mouse wallpaper and toss the beer can collection . . ." Spouse disappeared behind his book, the portrait of a defeated man. When I got in that spring housecleaning mood, even if only once a decade, he had no alternative but to sulk.

I made appointments for carpet and drapery cleaning and arranged a family work detail. Eldest was scheduled for a baseball team practice, but the rest of us forged ahead, sudsy spiderwebs falling in our faces and the teens chanting chain gang songs in the background. As we went, we made a pile of stuff to throw out in the center of the living room. "I suppose we should toss all of this on a backyard bonfire," I said as the work drew to a close.

But Daughter had a better idea. "Let's have a garage sale," she suggested.

"A garage sale?" her father repeated. "Strangers tramping across the crabgrass? Junk all over the driveway? Little tiny price tags? Not on your life!"

And so, on a beautiful April day, we set up tables, hung signs, and proudly displayed our junque. With visions of a cash windfall, kids who previously exhibited tortoise-like enthusiasm about cleaning their rooms had plowed through the upstairs ruins with a vengeance. No nook, cranny, or closet had escaped scrutiny; I had guarded them from ripping sheets off their beds (Daughter was astonished to discover that she *had* a bed) and unscrewing ceiling light fixtures.

"Can we sell this, Mommy?"

"My wedding ring? I don't think so, honey."

"How about this?"

"No, we may need the bathtub someday."

Within an hour everything not permanently anchored to the drywall had been toted to the driveway for pricing—a perfectly good pogo stick, three non-permanant-press tablecloths (I'd long ago donated my steam iron to my youngest sister, a Martha Stewart clone), several pounds of bread dough that had been in the freezer since 2007, all bits and pieces of my life. To the hordes that streamed up our walk, however, the items still had merit.

"Will you take a quarter for this dying poinsettia plant?" asked a rather aggressive woman, cornering my son. Did she know I was the neighborhood's black-thumb person and the plant was already living on borrowed time?

"I'll take this useless gold coin off your hands for half the asking price," a balding man accosted Husband.

"Well . . ."

Daughter, I noticed, had cleverly set up a chess game on a card table, positioning her brother and the dog on opposite sides. The match attracted a crowd, and the chess set sold right away. Unfortunately, the table did too; it was my best one and definitely *not* for sale. I also noticed that at least a thousand neighborhood children had visited our sale at nine a.m., run out of money at 9:15, and were now settled down in the driveway for the duration, making paths almost impassable for serious consumers. "Why don't you guys set up your own stands?" I suggested. "You can sell some of your toys or lemonade or . . ."

"Can I sell this, Mrs. A?"

"Bring your baby brother home, dear."

I left them to their dickering and slipped inside to run the snowblower through the rooms and complete my annual dusting. It was hard to recognize the place. Sterile. Immaculate. Junkless. Depersonalized. The walls and floors were gleaming, and the closets boasted plenty of storage space. We had disposed of all those wrappers from candy that was no longer manufactured, and even the lamp shade with the hole in it had been replaced. With the removal of the refrigerator magnets, I realized that the fridge had been green all these years and I had always assumed it was brown. It was certainly satisfying to be organized at last. So why did I feel that something ominous was taking place?

"Oh, there you are." Husband poked his head around the doorway. "Listen, there's a lady outside who wants to buy the front porch."

"I'm not sure I like this," I told him, waving my arms at the strangely spotless environment. "What have I done? Is this really our home?"

"Yes and no." He came to put a comforting arm around me. "It's just the end of one era and the beginning of another. "It's you and I getting ready for the rest of our lives. It's sorting out the old and making plans for the new. The new might be very nice, you know."

"I think you're right," I said as I leaned against him. "And we don't have to do anything drastic just yet, do we?"

"This is drastic enough," he agreed, staring at the matching lamp shades and color-coordinated dish towels. "Why don't we just admire it for a while?"

And that's what we did.

Eleven Ways to Survive Your Teen

Last week I was invited to give a how-to lecture on raising teenagers. The adolescent psychologist originally booked to speak had canceled at the last minute, since his adolescent had left the car on empty; I was the only alternative. Because I've written material on teenagers, people assume that I know something about them. In this instance, I dispelled that myth soon after I reached the podium. "I'm a normal befuddled mother like all of you," I reassured the audience. "See my gray strands, the tremor in my hands? I'm here because Betty, the program chairwoman, is a friend."

"I promised her a decent fee," Betty piped up.

"And it beats reruns," I added.

The audience was becoming disgruntled. "What can you tell us about our teenagers that will help us through it all?" asked a lady in the front row. She was wearing one red kneesock and one white one. Obviously she was a victim of her daughter's I'm-out-of-pantyhose-so-I'm-taking-your-last-pair syndrome.

"I need some *practical* advice," commented her neighbor as she shredded stale bread into a giant-sized plastic bag for turkey stuffing, although it was actually Easter next week, not

Thanksgiving. This mother had heard "Hey Mom, there's never anything to eat around here," and had decided to make a meal three times the normal size.

I took a deep breath. "Let me share my eleven tips," I suggested, "and then we can talk about anything I've left out.

1. Never send your teenager to the store in your car for a gallon of milk unless he knows he is not to make the trip via Milwaukee.

2. Under no circumstances should you enter your teen daughter's bedroom unless you are wearing an oxygen mask or have not seen your daughter in three days.

3. Understand that an adolescent's days and nights are suddenly reversed; he needs someone to tap-dance on his stomach at eight a.m., but he can stay up playing video games until dawn.

4. Consider purchasing transparent refrigerator and freezer doors to aid your son in his every-five-minute grocery inspection.

5. Consult your daughter before buying your own clothes. She may have strong moral objections to borrowing anything but cashmere sweaters and designer boots.

6. Develop a personal relationship with your plumber, since he'll be dropping by every three months to dislodge hairballs from your bathroom drain. Consider buying shampoo in five-gallon drums.

7. Be grateful for small favors. When your teenager says "What?," he is actually conducting a conversation with you. Especially intimate moments may include, "Who, me?"

8. Outsmart them. If you inform your daughter that you loathe her current boyfriend, she'll be going steady with

him by the weekend. If, instead, you ply him with pizza while murmuring wistfully about grandchildren, she'll drop him like a hot pastrami.

9. Refrain from throwing your son's iPod out the window just because he played the latest Metallica song 137 consecutive times. Instead, ask if he'll teach you the lyrics, as you'd like to sponsor a sing-along for the neighborhood.

10. Learn to ask yourself, "Will this matter in ten years?" If it won't (odd-colored hair, chaotic closet), ignore it. If it will (moral principles, respect for authority), stand firm.

11. Realize that teens may be frustrating, whiny, unpredictable, and messy, but someday justice will triumph. Someday they'll be parents too.

Concluding, I asked the audience if I'd left anything out. "Not a thing," said the woman with the multicolored socks. "What a relief to know I'm not the only mother living in an asylum."

Her companion hefted the bag of bread onto her shoulder. "Come on, Doris. Let's go have coffee and then shop for pantyhose. After all, we owe it to ourselves."

Next time maybe I'll talk about two-year-olds. The ages are actually very similar.

Youth would be an ideal state if it came a little later in life.

—Herbert Asquith

Absolutely Nothing to It

In years past, I was one of those extremely fortunate women whose physicians periodically ordered her into the hospital for minor repairs or tests. Including the births of my children, I averaged a medical mini-vacation almost once a year.

Most people, admittedly, do not regard hospital confinement as a "lucky break," and I will admit that two a.m. medication cups aren't as thrilling as lying on a tropical beach. But unexpected blessings frequently surfaced when I was absent from the home front, and I eventually recommended the practice to everyone under fifty. (The over-fifties have enough real physical problems to guarantee an occasional break.) If one did not have a genuine reason for hospital admission, one could hang around with a friend who was coming down with a plague or trip nonchalantly over a skateboard while Husband was there to notice, thus guaranteeing temporarily-out-of-service status. The bridge club, of course, was their usual understanding selves, promising not to approach the house or offer help to Husband in any way. That did not keep them from commenting on my situation.

"I hope you don't get that blasted tube down your throat," mused a new member to our choir's second alto section.

"Just remember to cough a lot," Penny reminded me, "no matter how much it hurts."

"It'll be a snap," my sister reassured me. "Remember how fast I bounced back?" I remember all right; she had a full-time housekeeper for three weeks afterward and still couldn't stand up straight until Christmas.

I usually scheduled one of my mini-vacations during spring break, when Husband would be stuck with childcare and domestic duties. Happily, my hiatus gave him the opportunity to put into practice all those housekeeping theories he frequently quoted. "Running a house is simply a matter of proper organization," he would assure me as I packed my suitcase. (Did I leave enough hot dogs? Tuna?) Eventually I squared my shoulders, kissed the kids (most of whom had to be dragged off the park swings to say good-bye), and clutched Husband's hand as he drove me to my date with destiny.

Entering a hospital is like moving to another planet. Nothing prepares one for the complete lack of privacy, much less a roommate or two who are farther along than you are in the healing process and want only to talk. You, of course, have brought along a suitcase full of bestsellers that you saved for your mini-vacation, and you now cannot get past chapter one, either because of a too-perky roommate or, in other cases, a roommate who had surgery a day ahead of you and whose moans offer a taste of what you'll be looking like and feeling just twenty-four hours from now.

How should I react if my roommate is in traction because she misread her *Introduction to Spinning Class* book, and insists on giving me a blow-by-blow account of her lawsuits against the publisher, the author, the gym owner, the class leader, and the leotard manufacturer? Is it against hospital rules to watch something *other* than a game show on daytime television? If a paramedic asks if he may "learn a little about IVs" by connecting mine, should I volunteer? Why, if I blink my eyes, will I miss the surgeon's daily visit?

Husband usually phoned only two or three times during my first evening as a patient, informing me that he had re-routed my carpools because I was wasting gas. (Men don't understand that when driving the kids' swim or baseball teams, one picks up the troublemaker *last*, and the one on our route lives next door.) My better half also wondered why there was a turtle in our bathtub and whether our sixth-grade daughter was really permitted to wear sequined eye shadow and stay out until three a.m. I would coach him, while marking my place in my romance novel with a chocolate bar.

"Nothing to it!" he'd report heartily during the next day's visiting hours, although I usually noted that he had not shaved and his eyes seemed strangely glazed. I told him each time that I was fortunate to be married to such a capable helpmate. He agreed.

By the following day the children would have phoned, filling me in on some minor details that Husband had forgotten to mention. I would learn of the thrilling fire-department rescue of Baby Sister from her locked second-floor bedroom. Second Son usually pointed out that since he was too young to join the Army, he saw no reason to live under the command of General George Patton. Two of the boys were apparently sleeping in the neighbor's hot tub, and the eight-year-old reported that all the clean laundry had been thrown on the dining room table. Because he hadn't located any underpants since Monday, he was thinking seriously of running away.

My across-the-street pal, ever vigilant, usually added an admiring tidbit, filling me in on how masterfully Husband dashed into supermarket-parking-lot traffic to rescue Baby Sister. Of course the shopping cart had overturned, all the eggs were broken, and Baby had left her shoes in the frozen-foods section.

"How's everything going?" I would query as Husband shuffled in to visit me.

"You women," he chuckled. "Always making such a big deal out of housework." He flopped onto the other bed and promptly fell asleep.

Checkout day dawned, and Husband arrived three hours early, pacing the hospital corridors while I waited to be released. Shoving me into the car before any medical personnel could change their minds, he typically made the journey home in record time, sounding the horn as we approached our driveway. Children came running from all directions. "Welcome home, Mommy!" They'd tumble into my waiting arms. "Can we *not* have pizza tonight?"

The house was welcoming too, freshly vacuumed and polished. No one but I would ever notice the newly mended dining room chair or the streaks on the wall left from an apparent grease fire. "You've done a grand job," I praised Husband. "But, be honest. What was it like to be Mommy for a week?"

"Seriously?"

"Uh-huh."

"It was like I had died and gone to hell. No hope glimmering in the distance that the dishes would ever keep up with the meals. I found myself praying that I'd be sent on a business trip to the Congo. I—"

"You don't have to tell me any more," I reassured him, throwing in an extra hug, as the benefits descend. There's nothing better for a wife than the opportunity to be missed.

And nothing better for a husband than to miss her.

Your wife shall be like a fruitful vine within your house, Your children like olive plants around your table.

—Psalm 128:3

A New Member of the Family

When our children were small, I would tiptoe into their bedrooms at night and pray over them. I would ask for health, safety, and strong spiritual faith, all the blessings mothers desire. Then I would pray for their future spouses. Although unknown to us, these little ones were already on earth, I reasoned. Someday they would be part of our family, and through the girls would come our grandchildren. I prayed that they were being raised in loving and stable homes, just like the one we were attempting to provide.

Years passed, our children grew, and one evening, our oldest son brought a girl home to dinner. Instantly, she seemed familiar to me. Since she had grown up a short distance away, I assumed I had met her parents or she had previously visited our home. (People enter and exit so frequently here that, in many cases, the friendships end before I get introduced. Today, for example, there's a boy in our family room working on a 5,000-piece puzzle. None of us has any idea who he is, and we suspect he may not know he's in the wrong house, but he's quiet, and I've never been able to finish that puzzle . . . but that's another story.) Anyway, although the new girl and I attempted to find a connection over the next few months, we finally concluded that our paths had never crossed.

One evening they both came in, flushed and happy. It had been a special night, rife with planning, and our son seemed somewhat uptight, rather than having his usual laid-back demeanor. Was something wrong? Or very, very right?

Yes! When the happy couple announced their engagement, we were delighted too, even though I knew that, for the mother of a groom, there are only two prerequisites: keep your mouth shut and wear beige. (I would probably fail both assignments.)

It was then I mentioned to my future daughter-in-law that I had been praying for her since my son was very young. "Oh!" Her face lit up. "*That's* why I've seemed so familiar to you. Our spirits recognized each other."

Of course. Our spirits. How could one person pray for another, especially for years, without eventually making a connection? I had looked for that link in the details of our outer lives. But instead, it had grown in our hearts, as most worthwhile things do.

I had not been alone in those darkened rooms. God Himself had been with me. And He would remain as our family began our next phase of life.

Thank you, Father, for bringing us this far. And really, must it be beige?

Excuse Me for Living

There's something about enrolling your youngster in middle school that brings a tear to the maternal eye. Not a tear of sentiment, mind you. My where-have-the-years-gone mourning takes place at the kindergarten door; from that point on, parenthood becomes a fun experience. (After all, the kids are absent regularly from the home front, and when they are present, can make their own sandwiches.)

No, the sorrow that accompanies this milestone of junior high registration stems from a different source. Junior high marks the time when our children shed their trusting, innocent Mommy-Is-Wonderful attitude, disengage from the closeness we once shared, and, seemingly overnight, turn into acid-tongued, critical know-it-alls whose prime purpose in life is to shape parents up.

It certainly starts innocently enough, just a snide remark now and then. In fact, when our first son reached this stage, I didn't notice it immediately. True, he didn't want to hold my hand anymore on our walks to the supermarket, but since he was almost my height by then, that was understandable. When he refused to be seen with me *anywhere* in public, however, I demanded to know why. My first mistake.

"It's not you." Son attempted diplomacy. "It's your Mom jeans."

5 1

"My what?"

"Those pants—they're up around your neck. Gross."

I stared down at the offending garment. "Well, I guess people do wear jeans a lot lower now . . . but they're so comfortable."

Son rolled his eyes.

Since I didn't want him to be a social outcast (and from the sound of it, my wardrobe was the reason he hadn't been invited to the Farrell party last weekend), I compromised. I bought a spiffy jogging outfit to wear on excursions past his school and a pair of four-inch heels to don at parent-teacher conferences (and to be removed as soon as the meeting ended and I found my car in the school parking lot).

It didn't do any good. I discovered a short time later that the real problem was my mouth. While driving several boys to basketball practice one evening, I had the audacity to take part in the backseat conversation. I actually said something witty, but instead of a few chuckles and "Oh, Mommy . . ." there was a shocked silence that lasted until the cargo had actually hit the gym door. News of my totally unacceptable behavior circulated around the cafeteria the next day; Son was so humiliated that he failed dribbling tryouts. It was my fault, of course, that he eventually made the second-string team instead of the varsity.

"When will you ever learn?" Husband chided me. "The chauffeuring rule is: eyes straight ahead, lips locked, and don't drive anything but a Humvee or foreign sports car."

"We don't *have* a Humvee or a foreign sports car."

"Precisely." Husband grinned. "They'll just have to walk." I was beginning to catch on.

By ignoring us at every opportunity (except on allowance day), Son eventually passed through middle school and became almost human again. Then it was Daughter's turn. My first lesson

with her came on the softball field, where I foolishly showed up
to watch her game.

"Great catch!" I shouted enthusiastically as she trotted by.

"Mother, please!" Daughter hissed. "Everyone's looking at
me!"

"Don't people usually watch the shortstop?" I inquired.

"And do you have to jump up and down whenever we score a
run? All the girls hate me. I wish I were dead. I'm so embarrassed."

"I'll try to restrain myself," I promised humbly.

"Never mind." Daughter sighed. "Did you remember to bring
the team treat?"

"Yes. Popsicles."

"Popsicles! They're *baby* treats! How could you? Oh, I'm
ruined."

The next week I decided to stay home from the game. Since
my mere existence was becoming a problem, I reasoned Daughter would probably play better without me.

"Hurry up, Mom. We're late," Daughter called as she ran by,
looking for her mitt.

"I'm not going," I informed her.

"Not going?" She stared at me in disbelief. "Oh, great. You
just don't care about me at all, do you?"

At this point, frankly, no. But that hasn't stopped Daughter
from caring about *me*. Due to her wise and constant counsel, I
have discovered that I wear the wrong color lip gloss (it makes
my skin look sallow), am at least a thousand pounds overweight,
and have hideous taste in books, music, movies, and friends. I
wonder how I've managed to bumble through life thus far. I'm
certainly glad she's here to monitor my every move. So glad, in
fact, that I've applied to a cloistered convent for admission—hers.

"That would be a rash move," Husband pointed out yesterday.

"Underneath all that orthodontia and frizz, she's really a nice person. Don't you want her to stick around so we can watch her grow out of this phase?"

"I'll be in the Holy Angels rest home by that time," I snapped. "Although on Monday we did make eye contact. Maybe there's hope."

"Mom!" Younger Son slammed into the room, face red. "Did you tell Mrs. Holmes that I got an A in Social Studies?"

"Sure did. I was so proud of you, and . . ."

"Oh, no! Now everyone will think I'm a wimp! How *could* you?"

How could I, indeed? He's just starting middle school.

Most children threaten at times to run away from home. This is the only thing that keeps some parents going.

—*Phyllis Diller*

Rating Your Marriage

Ever notice those cute pop-psychology quizzes in women's magazines or on the back of oatmeal boxes? You know the kind: "Would You Marry Him Again?" or "How to Decide if Your Partner Is Right for You." I've always hesitated taking them for fear of scoring in the bottom percentile, and then what would I do? Does it help to know that, according to the experts, I've made a really poor choice, especially if, for the past decade or so, the guy has been my best friend? (Okay, so I'm not saying anything about the first several years . . .)

Most of these quizzes are aimed toward the newly married, those who are just beginning to rub the stars from their eyes to grasp the reality of "till death do us part." Aside from retirement publications, which I don't yet read (at the rate we're going, who can possibly imagine life without a paycheck?), there don't seem to be many quizzes aimed toward those married couples with a bit of experience under their belts, who have put in enough pillow-talk time to regard the question "What is your mate's favorite gooey dessert?" as completely irrelevant to their happiness quotient. (For example, my mate—who just received the results of his cholesterol test—isn't permitted any desserts at all, much less gooey ones. And of course he's been married to me long enough to know that if he does want anything sinful and delicious, the Kitchen of Joan Marie is the last place to look.)

I've been thinking about it. Since I can't find a test for those in our special status, I'll devise one. If I can't bring myself to take it, it'll still be fun to see how well all our long-married pals are doing. Try it! Just circle the response that best reflects your relationship:

1. You regard your spouse as

    a. Your best friend and lover and favorite tennis partner.
    b. Someone you get along with most of the time because the alternative is too expensive and messy.
    c. Someone sent by God to test your spiritual growth.
    d. Depending on the weather, all of the above.

2. When you want your spouse's undivided attention, you

    a. Simply ask.
    b. Send the kids to Grandma's and cook his favorite gourmet dinner.
    c. Unplug the television during the middle of the Bears game while throwing your wedding ring at his head.
    d. Depending on the urgency of your need, all of the above.

3. You are most annoyed when your husband

    a. Buys you a stunning dress—two sizes too small! ("I just eyeballed it, hon.")
    b. Admires a member of the opposite sex in your presence (if you are in labor at the time, add thirty-seven points to your score).

    c.   Calls to say he's not coming home after work.

    d.   Calls to say he is coming home after work.

4.   You criticize your spouse

    a.   Only mentally, and while praying for him.

    b.   Only for major lapses, such as forgetting to pay the mortgage (as the realtors come up the front walk) or forgetting to bring the baby back from the pediatrician's office.

    c.   Only if you're venting to your mother.

    d.   Only over the public address system at the high school football stadium.

5.   You compliment your spouse

    a.   Often, and with actions to emphasize your words.

    b.   When he truly deserves it (you wouldn't want to spoil him).

    c.   Because it's a test of your spiritual growth.

    d.   Only during a full moon.

6.   When you and your spouse disagree, you

    a.   Talk out your differences pleasantly until you've reached a mutually agreeable solution.

    b.   Agree to disagree and refuse to hold a grudge (longer than tomorrow night).

    c.   Throw a temper tantrum.

    d.   Excuse yourself to go out for a short walk to clear the air—then keep going till you reach Cincinnati.

7.   You and your mate have probably remained together all these years because

a. You love each other deeply and can't imagine being apart.
b. You don't take your relationship for granted and are willing to work at it.
c. Neither of your mothers will let you come home.
d. Depending on the situation, all of the above.

Give yourself 4 points for each *a* answer; 3 points for each *b* answer, 2 points for each *c* and one point for each *d*. Add your score to determine the health of your marriage.

28–26   Impossibly healthy; you are probably in denial.

25–18   Pretty typical; keep trying.

17–8   In need of improvement; how about a just-the-two-of-you trip to Hawaii?

7 or less   Amazingly honest; you're a wonderful couple and truly deserve each other.

I love being married. It's so great to find that one special person you want to annoy for the rest of your life.

—*Rita Rudner*

Going to Harvard . . . or Someplace

There comes a day in every parent's life when the oldest child (who was in pull-ups only yesterday) is ready to choose a college. According to the experts who monitor such happenings, the move heralds a whole new life for the young adult. Few seem to notice that it heralds a whole new life for the young adult's parents too.

Choosing a college begins long before Son or Daughter (and fifteen duffel bags) is deposited at the dormitory door. It starts in the junior year of high school when Student is required to take admission tests and begin the selection process. (The kid who will make these earth-shattering decisions is the same one who only yesterday tossed ice cubes down his sister's T-shirt, who hasn't made his bed since he started T-ball, and whose favorite intellectual pursuit is watching *Happy Days* reruns.) Most teens are understandably confused about choosing a college, since there are so many factors to consider. How many days of vacation are scheduled? Is an eighteen-hole golf course (and greens fees) included in the tuition? Does the cafeteria feature homemade desserts? And, of course, are flat-panel televisions standard in all dorm rooms?

Perplexed beyond measure, most students eventually turn to

their parents for aid and comfort. So we of the older generation have to be prepared to advise them. That leads inevitably to the college visiting season, usually right after the results of the ACT and SAT placement test grades have been distributed. Since no school is right for every student, it's important for both parent and child to be aware of some do's and don'ts:

DO make finances a major consideration. There are always a few organized couples who started a college savings program around the time the first ultrasound was taken. Most of us, however, are too caught up in the day-to-day luxuries of life (food, shelter, and utilities) to think about future financial traumas until they arrive. "You can't be old enough for college," Husband once bellowed in shock. "Why, you're not even shaving yet."

"Dad, I'm a girl."

"And she wants to go to Harvard," I added proudly.

He paled, then swallowed hard. "Would the rest of the family be willing to quit eating for the next four years?" he asked the room at large. Since no one volunteered to make the supreme sacrifice, we discovered that our state university was more than adequate. The other kids in a family have to be considered too.

DON'T be alarmed at the more casual lifestyles now prevalent on campus. Since the Dark Ages, when you majored in the philosophy of colors and occasionally stayed out all night as an act of defiance that no one noticed, many things have changed. Boys seem to wander freely throughout girls' dorms, usually wearing a pair of basketball shorts and not much else. (It's only later that you realize they live there too.) The most common approved student hobby seems to be eating (directly out of cans), followed closely by napping, jogging, and drinking beer. All sorts of subversive-sounding groups have headquarters right next to the Dean's office, church services are often held at midnight, and no one seems to own a pair of shoes (other than flip-flops), including many of the professors. It's all part of the grand adventure, and despite parental misgivings, kids seem to adjust rather well.

DON'T expect much communication with your student until he runs out of cash. Collegiates are notoriously poor correspondents, preferring instead to text message, primarily during three a.m. dorm parties or minutes before they leave to come home on an unannounced visit. (You—if you have managed to decipher the text—will be expected to pick them up on a highway oasis fifty miles away "somewhere between six and eight, Mom, or later if the fuel pump stops working.")

DO comfort your starving student with plenty of care packages from home. You may be spending your retirement fund on Child's board bill, but he's still hungry all the time, and there's nothing that raises his spirits more than a goody-pack from Mom's kitchen. Ice cream, pizza, hard-boiled eggs, and green grapes don't pack well, but almost everything else does, including a new pair of jeans, a can of tennis balls, McDonald's coupons, and the latest SpongeBob video. Remember too that students never take all their belongings back to school with them, and about five hours after Collegiate has left home, you'll get a phone message saying, "I forgot my down jacket, Ma. Can you just toss it in a big envelop and mail it here by Friday?"

DON'T expect college to be a four-year package deal. Few eighteen-year-olds know what they want to be when they grow up. (Few forty-year-olds do either.) So the kids simply pick something that sounds reasonable, like Ukrainian dancing, and plunge ahead. Somewhere around junior year they discover that the job market in Ukraine is somewhat limited, and they decide that they would much rather major in techniques of racquetball instead. This shift requires that they go back and pick up all the required courses that they didn't take earlier. Which, in turn, can lead to college itself becoming a career. (At least you know where he's going to be during the next decade.)

DO know that saying good-bye will be harder than you expected. You have met your child's roommate, and you have gotten through the parents' orientation weekend (which at some colleges is now stretching into a third or fourth day, and will those parents please get a life); you have managed to move Child into the dorm (on the twenty-seventh floor in a one-elevator building), and it's time to say good-bye. "Don't go!" Suddenly you want to say it out loud. "There is too much waiting out there for you, and we cannot protect you from it all . . ." But you do not speak, of course. Mothers know how to examine a fallen leaf or high-flying plane to hide the tears in their eyes. We have done it for so many years, at so many doors . . . And perhaps the children never know.

Soon, all too soon, we'll be facing empty nests (and full refrigerators). For now, our job is to stand by, encourage, support, and love our young adult as he finishes life in our care. Just in time for the next child to ask, "Dad, can I go to Harvard?"

The invention of the teenager was a mistake. Once you identify a period of life in which people get to stay out late but don't have to pay taxes, naturally no one wants to live any other way.

—*Judith Martin*

The Fabric of Life

This is a good idea," my friend Sandy said one morning, reading an announcement posted in the back of church. One of the parish committees was sponsoring a raffle for a child who needed costly cancer treatments. "We should make a quilt with the neighbors and donate it as a prize to the raffle."

"I think you're out of your mind," I told her loyally, "and you know I haven't sewn anything since I took up the hem on my school uniform."

"As I recall, you stapled that hem." Sandy and I go back a long way. "But you could thread needles for the rest of us—and pour coffee."

I was the only reluctant one, for she won over several neighborhood women. And so, meeting every Thursday evening, we brought pieces of our own leftover sewing projects to join with others'. There were eleven of us, all ages and levels of sewing competence, and hardly anyone had ever made a patchwork quilt. But two of our members assured us that they knew enough to take gentle charge of it all. So, with our chairs pulled comfortably into a circle, we stitched.

And as our needles moved, something else began to happen too.

At that time, we lived in a neighborhood of Chicago apartments. Despite most of us having been there for several years, we had never developed close ties with one another. Our busy lives, jobs, and child-rearing had precluded meaningful companionship. A quick over-the-back-fence wave or a brief "hello" at the supermarket was as intimate as we'd become. Sandy and I, the only ones with preschool children, had sustained our friendship mainly out of need for adult camaraderie.

But now, as we laid aside some time each week for our joint mission, we began to view each other in a different way. Part of it was the unusual atmosphere, a quiet and relaxing evening oasis after our harried days. There was something restful about the soft, rhythmic work that encouraged communication.

At first we talked in general terms, commenting on the price of pot roast or the new houses at the end of the block. And then one evening Mrs. Wilson, a middle-aged woman who always seemed crabby when Sandy and I walked past her bungalow, picked up a scrap of red-and-white percale. Tears filled her eyes. "I remember this material," she murmured. "It's part of a dress I made for my daughter, Nan, when she was ten."

There was a sudden uneasy silence, and I blundered into it. "I didn't know you have a daughter, Mrs. Wilson," I said.

"I don't. Not anymore." Her words were stark. "She died four years ago, of leukemia."

We sat as if frozen. Then one woman reached over and took Mrs. Wilson's hand. "Nan was such a darling girl," she said. "You must have some wonderful memories."

Mrs. Wilson's tears ran slowly down her cheeks while the rest of us held our breath. "Why yes, I do," she said slowly. "There was the time . . ." Her words were hesitant at first. Then, as we listened intently, she went on, reliving the special moments, savoring the joy that a beloved child had brought to her.

Slowly other women added their memories of Nan Wilson—the bouncy brown ponytail, her first date, graduation with honors from college . . . How long, I wondered as I poured coffee for Mrs. Wilson, had she kept her grief bottled up because no one had offered her the opportunity, the time, the loving permission to express it? Perhaps she was "crabby" with Sandy and me because our strollers reminded her of her loss. Now, cocooned in the comfort of everyone's support, she was able to experience that blessed release, add Nan's scrap of red-and-white, and begin to say good-bye.

From that day on, the quality of our relationships changed. As barriers came down, we began to share our inmost concerns. Older mothers voiced worries about teenagers away at college; would solid family values go with them or would they be vulnerable to other, less suitable ways of life? An elderly widow confided her desire to remain independent during her last years. Sandy and I released our frustrations over endless diapers and toddler demands.

We talked of God and faith, of the meaning of life, of goals, plans, and dreams. And we laughed—healing laughter all the more precious because it was shared. We learned the importance of needing others, allowing our weaknesses to show so that others might console us, receiving as well as giving. As our quilt took shape, so too did our lives. Never again would we be too rushed, too caught up in trivial matters to touch another.

The day came when our quilt was finished, and together we went to deliver it. The woman in charge of the raffle was astonished when we told her how it had been made. "All of you?" she asked. "All sewing together?"

All of us. "And we're going to make another," Sandy declared. "We need the therapy!"

Mrs. Wilson and I shared a special smile as everyone laughed, then we watched as the quilt was folded and carefully packaged. Yellow corduroy, blue-and-white gingham, pink-dotted dimity, Nan's red-and-white percale—the fabrics of our lives now forever linked. It had started as a work for charity. But the quilt had made us rich.

Lord,
In our world of instant everything,
Help me to remember that relationships take time,
And that I need to sharpen mine.
I praise you for the friends you've placed into my life.
Bless them for their investments in my life. Amen.

—Angel of Hope Ministry

Not Just Yet

It's that time of year again. My husband and I are celebrating our birthdays. Having a birthday was once a relatively innocent pastime. There'd be candles, a cake, and gifts handmade by the children (usually colorful potholders, as I recall). Sometimes a few friends joined the merry-making and well-wishing. One's new age, it seemed, held no greater consequence than the old one had.

Then Husband hit the magic number—forty-five. A few days later he received a congratulatory letter from our park district trustees and, instead of his usual pool pass, a Bronze Card entitling him to 10 percent off of diving board and sauna privileges because "you are one of our most treasured assets, a Senior Swimmer."

My husband peered at the Bronze Card in disbelief. "A Senior Swimmer?" he croaked. "Just because I have to put on my glasses to read the concession stand billboard? Just because there was that incident with the paramedics . . . ?"

"There, there," I soothed. "I'm sure lots of people doze off while they're floating . . ."

"Okay, so I'm a little absentminded lately, but I remembered your name tonight, didn't I?"

"On the second try," I acknowledged.

"How can I be considered a senior *anything* when we still have a child in middle school?" He looked around vaguely. "We do, don't we?" I nodded. "They're treating me like a . . . a relic!" he sputtered.

"You're far too sensitive," I pointed out. "It's merely one way society acknowledges and honors your maturity. Besides, it's going to save us money!"

This was the wrong approach, I realized belatedly as Husband stomped out of the room. Economics had never been his strong suit. For years I'd begged him to fill in his check stubs, to no avail. He still doesn't know the names of the mutual funds we own and thinks Ginny Mae is my bridge partner. And when I delightedly discovered that, in addition to wisdom, Husband's advancing age entitled him to a 15 percent discount on matinee movie tickets, reduced rates on haircuts, and—if we wanted to eat before four thirty on Thursdays—a price break at the local diner, my spouse was not impressed. "*You* get on the bus and ask those adolescent drivers for the senior discount," he challenged from behind the editorial page. "I dare you!"

"I can't," I reminded him sweetly. "I don't qualify yet."

But I knew how he felt. Everyone did seem to be getting younger. Our daughter's biology teacher wore orthodontia, my internist carried her stethoscope in her backpack . . . But why should mere male ego stand in the way of consumer savvy?

The breakthrough finally came when Husband passed yet another significant birthday—one that qualified him for reduced hotel rates. Added to those bargain airfares, it made our longed-for trip to the Grand Canyon a distinct possibility. "With our discounts, we could stay in luxury quarters for the same price we'd usually pay at Ed's Motel and Lawncare," I explained.

Slowly he lowered the newspaper. "Hmm . . ."

"And with your senior restaurant markdowns and weekday tour specials . . ."

"You've convinced me," Husband sighed. "I guess aging has its rewards too. Maybe I ought to start taking advantage of them. Let's visit a travel agent."

I *knew* he wouldn't let a silly little thing like vanity cloud his common sense. It had taken some time to adjust, of course, but from then on, I felt sure he would be suavely flashing his Bronze Card at the slightest opportunity . . .

The travel agent, who appeared to have recently graduated from eighth grade, seated us graciously. "A trip to the Grand Canyon?" she cooed. "How delightful! And will you be using your senior discounts?"

Complacently I waited for Husband to answer, waited until a sinister little quiver started in my stomach. The agent wasn't looking at Husband. She was looking at *me*.

We do, of course, intend to visit the Grand Canyon as soon as we retire and have the time to do it right. But as I told Husband yesterday, why rush it? Honestly, some people will do anything to save a few dollars.

Grey hair is a crown of glory,
It is gained by virtuous living.

—Proverbs 16:31.

Love, Joan

Dear Aunt Margo,

I was thrilled to receive your dear invitation asking our whole gang to accompany you this summer on your vacation. I imagine the kids would have a marvelous time on a hippopotamus hunt, and there's certainly nothing I'd enjoy more than sifting through archaeology digs, guessing whether the pottery chips are one or two million years old (I've had a lot of experience with sand). But reluctantly, we'll have to pass on the expedition—there just isn't enough in the petty cash fund to finance a trip to Africa. Actually, given the gas prices lately, we're just hoping for enough fuel to make it out of town.

As you guessed, we're all hard at work trying to decide where we should travel. (And how. And sometimes even why.) I originally suggested a visit to my sister's in Minneapolis, since we could save money by sleeping in her wine cellar. Your nephew roundly vetoed this suggestion, claiming there's nothing exciting to do in Minneapolis, and considering that the mosquito is the official state bird there, I ended up agreeing with him. Instead he has volunteered a rather unique suggestion—we are to spend the summer painting the garage, weeding the lawn, and, as an occasional break in the monotony, removing a dead tree or two. I fail to see how this can be considered a break in our routine and have, quite naturally, refused to consider it. As a result, Husband is sleeping in the aforementioned garage. I would appreciate any and all suggestions for breaking this deadlock.

Best wishes as you prepare for your latest safari, Aunt Margo, and we'll be with you in spirit. It's so exciting to have an explorer in the family—you have no idea how the kids' neighborhood status rises each time they receive your letters bearing those funny foreign stamps. I don't know where you get your energy— by the time I'm eighty-five like you, I'll probably desire nothing more strenuous than an occasional round of Chinese Checkers . . .

Love,
Joan

* * *

May 20

Dear Aunt Margo

Glad to hear you arrived safely in Africa, and your unexpected skirmish with the boa constrictor at the airport sounds too exciting for words! How I wish we were there to share it all.

No, we haven't decided where (or if) we are traveling this summer. Between the local skateboard competition and the annual Park District Potholder exhibit, my time is already being whittled away. And of course our teenagers greet every suggestion with a one-word comment: "Gross." If they had their way, we'd spend the next few months at a nonstop skateboard competition, provided it offered an unlimited supply of pizza. Then there's the question of Little Sister—is she mature enough to accompany us on a tour of the Second World War Memorial museum? Or should the rest of us stifle our yawns and spend the day at Kiddieland? It's a real predicament, and no reasonable solution will be discarded!

Enjoy your upcoming trek into the pygmy village—we'll be holding our breath till we see the photos . . .

Love,
Joan

* * *

May 29

Dear Aunt Margo,

So good to get your letter, and I really appreciate your suggestion that I solve our vacation dilemma by packing Little Sister up and sending her on to you. Then the rest of us, as you pointed out, could spend a week enjoying adult pursuits such as sleeping an eight-hour stretch and renting movies whenever the spirit moved us.

Bless you for your thoughtfulness, and I do realize that Sister would get a kick out of seeing her first lava explosion, but I guess I'm still rather overprotective. Let's wait another year until she knows her name and telephone number, or at least until she stops dragging that moldy blanket along on every outing.

Our vacation plans are starting to jell—we've narrowed possibilities to a three-day barge cruise down the Mississippi River (including a stopover at a popcorn factory in southern Iowa) or attending the barbershop quartet semifinals in Kansas. I'll keep you informed.

Love,
Joan

* * *

June 8

Dear Aunt Margo,

The children received their tribal masks yesterday, and it was just too good of you. There were at least thirty neighbors in our backyard waiting to try them on, and someone from the local newspaper came to take photos ("A Little Bit of Africa Hits Suburbs"). Naturally I felt duty-bound to play the role of super-hostess, so after our summer supply of Popsicles had vanished from the freezer, I lit up the old barbeque and started on hot dogs. Well, wouldn't you know—one of the toddlers from across the street, fleeing in terror from that medicine man mask (the one with all the snakeskins hanging from it) crashed into the barbeque, and as it fell, it set fire to the garage. The firefighters were here in no time to put out the small blaze (three of them hung around afterward to have a turn wearing the masks). But obviously, considering the deductible on our home insurance, our summer vacation plans have (you'll excuse the expression) gone up in smoke.

I really don't mind. I'd spent all last week trying to fit three sets of golf clubs, an expectant cat, a tricycle, and a giant-sized freezer into the SUV and still have room for luggage and people. Now I won't have to worry about it.

Hurry home, Aunt Margo. We're dying to see your photos, especially the one of you swinging through the jungle Tarzan-style. Some people have all the luck!

Love,
Joan

Distant relatives are the best kind, and the further the better.

—Kin Hubbard

Everyone Else's Father

We women have heard all about "everyone else's mother" from our children (and from Dr. Phil). She's that paragon of virtue who models for Teen Magazine, puts up her own aluminum siding, bakes wheat bread, and speaks French fluently. But did you know that, according to the kids, "everyone else's father" also exists? In honor of Father's Day, I feel obliged to publicize this fellow, although we've never met.

From what I hear, "everyone else's father" is on a physical par with George Clooney—just over six feet tall, with a flat stomach, a full head of hair, and all his own teeth. He can run a five-minute mile and used to play for the Chicago Cubs yet is tactful enough to let his middle-school son win their daily free-throw contests. He can give piggyback rides to two daughters at the same time and generously lets them take his Olympic gold medals to school for show-and-tell.

(He never needs to be resuscitated by the paramedics after cleaning out the gutters or taking the dog for a romp.)

"Everyone else's father" is president of a large corporation that sends its executives on frequent trips to Disney World or Hawaii (and, of course, he loves taking his family along). He earns enough to keep all his offspring in the lap of luxury: not only the basic necessities—orthodontia, personal DVD players, and designer jeans—but also the niceties: a private room and bath for everyone over the age of twelve and individual sports cars for his teenagers. EEF is listed in Who's Who and is thinking about putting in a swimming pool. He would run for the Senate this year but hates to give up those lucrative consultant-to-the-president fees.

(He never stomps through the house waving a fistful of over-due bills and cutting up all the credit cards.)

I hear that "everyone else's father" has time for everything. He regularly volunteers at a local soup kitchen, runs the parish building drive, and coaches girls' soccer. He manages to spend one hour of quality time with each of his children every day, and is always available to take his wife dancing. He never needs to read a road map, keeps up with the current best sellers, and painted the living room in a single day so it would be ready for a bridal shower that evening.

(He never asks, "What day is it?," "Where are we going?," or "Whose children are these?")

EEF is broad-minded. He doesn't believe in a major time out just because the toddler broke an egg on his best designer suit ("She didn't mean it") or in taking the five-year-old home from the zoo because he's having a major meltdown in the reptile house. If the sixth grader wishes to experiment with dynamite (or keep fishing worms in the freezer), that's okay with him. And of course the teens are free to make up their own minds about R-rated movies, smoking weed, and whether to attend Sunday services. Usually they do, because EEF is a deacon at church and gives awesome and relevant sermons.

(He never stands in the middle of the kitchen and bellows, "Hey, everybody! This is not a democracy!")

"Everyone else father" doesn't get uptight about possessions. He smiles tolerantly when discovering his favorite hammer rusting in the weeds, his sterling silver cufflinks being used as game pieces, and his tuxedo and wallet borrowed for prom night. He buys more socks when the teens abscond with his supply, buys another sports magazine when the baby teethes on the current issue, and buys another house when the sixth grader's dynamite experiment gets a bit out of hand. Of course, he wouldn't dream of taking a bite out of the toddler's sandwich or using his daughter's motorcycle without permission.

(He never wraps a bedspread around his two-pound box of fudge, hides it in the back of his closet, and chuckles softly, "That'll fix 'em.")

"Everyone else's father" is kind and sensitive. He keeps his head when the sump pump backs up, and if Daughter has five D's on her report card, he gently discusses the situation with her and helps her understand that it isn't her fault. He dictates a term paper for the freshman (complete with bibliography and footnotes) and wouldn't dream of setting a curfew for the older teens. And when the garbage men mistakenly crush the toddler's doll house just because she carelessly left it at the curb on pickup day, he quietly builds her another.

(He never comes home from work and locks himself in the garage to listen to talk radio all evening.)

We hear about "everyone else's father" all the time, but I've yet to discover who he is or where he lives, which is probably a blessing. We mere mortals might have trouble living up to all that perfection.

I think, instead, we'll keep the harried, confused-but-always-trying head of the household that we have now. He may be last year's model, but we love him just the way he is.

A father is someone who carries pictures in his wallet where his money used to be.

—Unknown

Where Do the Pounds Go When You're Not Paying Attention?

Being slim all of my life, I took it for granted. Then several years ago I stopped smoking and gained twelve pounds. The twelve pounds were obviously meant for someone else; they were, in fact, the perfect example of a hostile takeover. But while I was trying to find out who owned them, they settled cozily around my hips, making jeans uncomfortable and my midriff a bit obvious. What was I going to do? Our eldest was getting married next year, and I had my heart set on a particular dress that probably didn't come in my current size . . .

Pleased as he was about my nonsmoking status, my physician was no help. "The weight is yours, all right," he counseled jovially. "Women tend to gain as they age. Twelve pounds are nothing to worry about."

"But what if I don't stop gaining?" I asked. (I could be a size 90 by the wedding if this kept up.)

He cleared his throat. "Well . . ."

Have you ever wondered where extra weight comes from, and where it goes when it's no longer yours? I would have asked the doctor about this, but he was already reaching for the doorknob.

"Your twelve pounds are nothing more than the inevitable middle-aged spread," my bridge club concurred knowingly as they passed chips and dip. "Accept them, get to love them, and enjoy life."

"But wearing the wardrobe I own is enjoyable too." I countered.

They shuffled cards. "Well . . ."

(Yes, it's fun to buy new clothes occasionally, but what if I lose again, and then gain again . . .) Counting calories was probably the ultimate answer, but I decided to do that later, maybe when all the kids left home and I could stock the refrigerator exclusively with kale and cabbage leaves.

Of course, I could join a health spa, again, but all the women there seemed to be size sixes. (Why would they have to exercise?) On the first morning of Beginner Body Rhythm last year, a gang of us were lined up in the gym hallway when suddenly a strange woman clutched my arm. "Look!" she croaked in horror, staring into the gym where everyone in the class, all wearing professional-looking leotards (most of us were in faded capris and socks) was somehow balancing on one elbow while the rest of their bodies arched precariously into thin air. The expression of stoic suffering on their sweaty faces was something to behold. "Oh no," sighed my companion. "We're not going to do *that*, are we?"

"That's the advanced group," I tried to comfort her. "And I think it's an optical illusion." But she was already halfway down the hall. I'll say this for her—she could really run.

I've tried that too—running, I mean. It's supposed to be good for your heartbeat, although I have always suspected that if I kept it up for more than a minute or two, I wouldn't have a heartbeat. Under exceptional circumstances, I am willing to run—down to the basement if a tornado actually comes (not just a warning siren) or over to the mall if there's a sale on silver jewelry. Beyond that, however, a brisk walk is about the best I can muster.

My current collegiate, a physical fitness buff, wasn't willing to watch me capitulate. "Mom, that's what you need to do," he unexpectedly commented one morning while filling a twenty-four-ounce glass with orange juice. "Walk."

"Walk?" I stared as if he were speaking in tongues. "I do walk."

"From the laundry room to the kitchen." He rolled his eyes. "I'm talking outside, Mom, that space between the back door and the car. You know, the rest of the world—trees, sidewalks, barking dogs."

This was the longest conversation I recalled having with this son since his grade school graduation, so I decided to appear interested. "Can I do it in denim or does it require a uniform?"

"Last I heard, the only necessity is a good pair of shoes." Son glanced at my flip-flops. "They should stay on your feet too."

"Will it make me thin again?"

"I don't know," he shrugged. "What have you got to lose?"

Twelve pounds, actually. But it was early spring. That evening, after the dinner dishes were done, I took Son's advice. (He, I noticed, took my car. Was this a ploy?)

Surprise number one was that I could cover a mile and a half (just around three reasonably long blocks) in about twenty minutes. Why had I assumed it would take all day? I added another block to my route, which took me by the tennis courts (where people who looked otherwise sane were spending inordinate amounts of time chasing a small green ball around a fenced-in area) and stepped up the pace, still finishing in about half an hour. A small time commitment for a vastly improved lifestyle.

For that was surprise number two. Despite my negative expectations, I actually began to enjoy the nightly trek. There was something soothing in the ritual of leaving behind family confusion, a blaring TV, and a jangling phone, and entering a quiet oasis where I could be alone with my thoughts and launch meaningful discussions with God. No one seemed to miss me, anyway, and as long as I pretended that the walk was a penance (sighing and groaning as I put on my shoes), no small child asked to be taken along. I grew calmer on the home front when faced with the usual plumbing disasters and emails from teachers, confident that however difficult the day, that gentle evening respite awaited me.

I felt better too. The rhythmic step-step and deeper breathing that are part of a brisk walk worked unexpected wonders on my rusty joints and lungs. In a subtle way, I experienced fewer aches, increased endurance, deeper sleep, an overall sense of well-being, inner peace—and was it my imagination or did my skin take on a warmer glow?

I walked through spring rains, summer sunsets, and the comforting crackle of autumn leaves. And when it was time for my annual checkup, I walked to the doctor's office. "You look wonderful," he enthused. "A new brand of cosmetics?"

"Just my usual radiance," I acknowledged. "And since our eldest took the bathroom scale to college, can we get the weigh-in over? Then I'll tell you all about it."

We stared at the dial. "Twelve pounds," I whispered. "I lost twelve pounds this year. And I never did go on a diet."

"I'd say you're definitely fooling Mother Nature," the doctor observed. "Want to let me in on the secret?"

I left him frowning thoughtfully (where *does* the weight go?) and walked home quickly. I could hardly wait to tell Son, and the bridge club, all about it. (And try on the dress.)

Reason to smile: Every seven minutes of every day, someone in an aerobics class pulls a hamstring.

—Unknown

Rate the Parents

I can't do the dishes now, Mom, I'm going to work." Twelve-year-old Daughter passed me briskly in the hall.

I've heard every excuse imaginable. "Let me explain something to you, sweetheart. Dishes *are* work—at least they were the last time I looked. And you're too young for anything fancier or better paying."

"Mother-r-r, please!" Daughter rolled her eyes. "I'm a babysitter, remember? And we have a union meeting tonight."

"A babysitters' union? What do you do there?"

"Like, we rank the families, of course."

"Rank the families? How?"

"Mother-r-r, please. Like whether they have movie channels and speed-dialing, and what kind of snacks they leave, or whether they leave any at all. Mostly we talk about the kids. Like, you know, how many, and whether they're potty-trained or go to bed early or are funny or bratty or know how to play computer games . . ."

My mouth dropped. "You mean . . ."

"We assign a rating code, just like they do with movies." Having warmed up, she was now almost speaking in full sentences. "With points for different categories. Like, the parents that have the most points get any sitter they want. The lower-point people have to get on a waiting list."

She bounced out, leaving me with my mouth still open. Times had certainly changed. I recalled my own babysitting days; true, I had been a casual preteen, tossing toddlers onto the slides at the corner park with mad abandon, racing a friend of mine, also babysitting, to see which of our occupied strollers would get to the corner first. And admittedly, I had spent a great part of my evening jobs talking on the phone, watching TV, and doing homework. But none of my small charges ever ate poison, flooded the bathroom, or woke up at night. (After our evening wrestling matches, they seemed to sleep the sleep of the exhausted.)

My perspective changed, of course, after I became a parent. The first thing to go was my nonchalant attitude. I checked out prospective sitters with the precision of a CIA agent, requiring references from Teen's bank, a chat with her mother, a demonstration of the proper way to change a diaper and wash a chubby little face. Having settled on a likely prospect, I then posted the telephone numbers of doctor, dentist, grandmother, neighbors living within a five-block radius, fire station, poison control center, and clergy, then spent the bulk of the night worrying about or phoning the home front. When we'd approach our house after an evening out, I'd check the nearby streets for police cars or ambulances (perhaps the sitter was hosting a frenzied group of Freddie Krugers in our absence). If all seemed normal, I would burst dramatically through the front door in an attempt to catch Sitter actually sleeping on the job. (Never mind that we were home a few hours later than we'd planned.) And if Sitter, instead, greeted me with a bright smile, folded her Social Studies notes, and assured me that the kids were "darling, absolutely well-behaved, Mrs. A," I still dropped her measly wage into her hand, directed her toward Mr. A's idling car, then sped into the bedrooms to see for myself whether my tots had dried strawberry jelly on their faces or appeared to be sedated.

Finally, deciding to keep Sitter, I would then provide her with lots of grocery snacks, bribe my kids to be nice to her (using the same grocery snacks), allow her to have a girlfriend over (after, of course, putting the friend through the same interview process), and invite her aunts to my cosmetics demonstration parties. If Sitter had small brothers and sisters, I would send each a Christmas gift, on the hopeful theory that they would one day grow up and step into the void that Sitter left when she had the nerve to get a better-paying job, go away to college, or get married. And yes, I had to admit it. My friends and I, in addition to rating recipes, beauticians, and pediatricians, also exchanged opinions on the merits of our sitters.

Eventually my own offspring—after distinguishing themselves as reliable newspaper delivery persons—had all moved on to became sitters, and when they were on duty, I was too, although no one seemed to notice until an emergency occurred. "No, don't give the baby cola," I once counseled a "sitting son" phoning at one a.m. from a house ten miles away. "Isn't there a bottle of formula in the refrigerator? Go and look."

Silence (except for the baby's screams) for what seemed like hours. Then, "Mom? You were right. There was a bottle of formula. I just dropped it."

During the summers, our gang enjoyed caddying at the local golf course, but that came to a halt when school began again. As soon as our eldest reached the magic age of sixteen, fast-food chains then became part of our heretofore uneventful lives. Working over a hamburger grill can be a fun experience for any teen, except for one problem: Fast-food chains, it seems, only need kids to work through the dinner hour, usually five to seven p.m. This situation wasn't too bad except that Oldest Son didn't yet have his driver's license. Good old Mom was thus required to put *our* dinner on hold in order to fight rush hour traffic to deliver Son to his waiting spatula, only to retrieve him when the supper rush dwindled.

The situation got more interesting the following year when Second Son turned sixteen and was given grill duty between four and six p.m. Eldest had his license by now but couldn't use the car because Second Son had to be transported (I wonder by whom?) an hour earlier. The clan on the home front grew noticeably thinner while waiting in vain for an evening meal. By the time I reported the burger-scheduling manager to the Better Business Bureau, our third child had a job too, as an usher at a nearby racetrack (where I would pick him up as the last contest started in order to beat the crowd.)

Clothes too played a part in the job arena. Through the years, our kids worked as movie ushers (black pants, white shirt, flashlight), checkout folks and waiters (maroon uniform, double-starched), snow-shovelers (anything lined with fur), and office boys (anything but jeans, which in itself is an interesting concept). On one memorable day, my oldest son (wearing the appropriate uniforms) caddied for, served lunch to, and took the movie ticket of the same man. I understand he is still talking about it. Since garb must be clean and dry in time for the next shift (shifts seemed to change as often as my moods), I usually spent more time talking to my washing machine than I ever did talking to my gang.

And now the kids' kids were rating the adults. It was startling and hard to accept. "I've been thinking," I told Daughter as she returned from her union meeting, "should you be putting material things ahead of a family's need for a sitter? Is that really a Christian concept? After all . . ."

"Like, relax, Mom." Daughter patted my head. "You know I usually only sit for the Bradfords, the Bradys, and the O'Briens. We all get along fine, and . . ."

"Then what's all this about a union?"

"Respect, Mom. Even kids need it, you know."

Like, sometimes she does make sense.

There's nothing wrong with teenagers that reasoning with them won't aggravate.

—*Unknown*

And the Lion Shall Lie Down with the Lamb

Last week our smaller gerbil, Ping, somehow escaped from her cage. While her companion, Pong, slept cozily under a layer of chewed-up newspaper, Ping explored the second floor and eventually ended up in one of the heating ducts. The kids, of course, had absolutely nothing to do with this happening; they were all busily engaged in some worthwhile activity—shoveling snow, doing homework, reciting the rosary, or figuring out how to improve their manners. But when Ping's absence was discovered, hysteria reigned. "Mom, you've got to do something!" was the general (screaming) consensus.

I could think of a lot of things I wanted to do, the most appealing being to pack a duffel bag and leave. But because my for-better-or-worse vow also includes the children, I hung in there and, with a combination of Cheerios for bait, a fish net, and a call to the current college kid for advice, I managed to coax Ping to safety. The kids cheered, of course, but when I looked in the mirror and discovered that the day's adventure had left me with even more gray hair, I wondered (again) why a presumably sane female like me would become housemother to so many furry and winged creatures.

In the beginning, as scripture points out, God made the birds of the air, the fish in the sea, and all the animals on the earth. But did he necessarily make them for *me*? At birth, was each species given a note directing him or her to our address with orders to take up residence there? If so, why?

Then again, perhaps I brought it on myself. After all, it started innocently enough several years ago with a pair of gold-fish our four-year-old won at a carnival when I wasn't looking. How much trouble can a few fish be?

The goldfish actually were no trouble (one helpfully died that very night when Four took it to bed with him). The problem came with all the fish accessories we needed to provide: large tank, filter, colored stones, marbles, castle, and paddle wheel—all so necessary for our finny friend's comfort. By the time the second goldfish went to that great big pond in the sky, this newfound hobby was claiming a larger share of the budget than groceries. And that was just the beginning.

Our next wildlife companion was a baby rabbit (at least she looked like a baby) our sixth-grader rescued from a secure nest. Rabbit Ruth Ann settled comfortably in a box near our space heater, endured the kids' petting and questions, but refused to eat the variety of raw vegetables we offered every hour. A few days later we discovered that Ruth Ann had no doubt been suffering from a belated case of morning sickness since her box now con-tained five more *very* small rabbits.

By this time our house consisted of Husband, myself, five kids, six new fish, Ruth Ann and her brood, and a canary we were temporarily boarding for my sister. Eventually by threatening to torch the kitchen, I persuaded the family to donate Ruth Ann and her offspring to a nearby nature center. No one spoke to me for two weeks, but the peace was heavenly.

I should have learned my lesson at this point, but no—some of us are slow. Our next pet was an ordinary puppy a former friend bestowed on us one afternoon when I was at a committee meeting. Said friend immediately left town, so I was unable to ask any questions about Pepper or what that thing that looked like a cage actually was. (I later discovered that it was a cage. Who knew?) Pepper seemed harmless enough, and the kids were ecstatic. They fought over who would walk him, who would feed him, whose bed he would grace each night. The quarrels went on for four days, at which point the novelty wore off, and Pepper became my dog.

Pepper and I passed the next week in a state of tentative compromise: he agreed to stay off the carpets if I would honor his two a.m. compulsion for the outdoors. Since our most recent baby had just started sleeping through the night, I thought this was a bit inconsiderate of Pepper. But being too tired to do anything about it, I braved the elements each night until Pepper went to the vet for his first exam.

"A nice dog," the vet proclaimed. "A bit small for a Great Dane, but he'll catch up."

"A what?" I asked, numb. "I thought Pepper was a terrier or something."

He shot me a withering glance, and so did Pepper. "Not a chance. This fellow will be bigger than your husband one day."

The new owners could send me a snapshot, I decided, and escorted Pepper back to my friend's house (there's the true meaning of friendship—the woman who will take her puppy back). This time, no one spoke to me for four weeks. I had time to finish three mystery novels before the kittens arrived.

At this point, it's safe to say that I'm having second thoughts about our wild kingdom. With the tadpoles temporarily occupying the bathtub (fish are again in the fish tank), Ping and Pong, and our poor abandoned canary (my sister never showed up), it's getting crowded around here. Not to forget the outdoors menagerie—a raccoon taking up residence in the garage, Jack the red squirrel who has gotten so cheeky over the past few seasons that he now peers through our kitchen door each morning, paws against the screen, waiting for some leftover toast. Right behind Jack is usually a family of chipmunks, wrestling and kidding around with each other as they wait for the leftover leftovers.

Kids can learn a lot from pets, but parents can learn even more. My lesson involves four simple words that I'm practicing faithfully and intend to use at the very next opportunity: "The lion may someday lie down with the lamb," I will announce, "but *not in my house.*"

A family is a unit composed not only of children but of men, women, an occasional animal, and the common cold.

—*Ogden Nash*

Here Come the Nuts!

● ●

*O*ne *May* evening, a new family, transferred from California onto Hickory Avenue, came by our house to say hello. They were all wearing in-line skates. "You must have a lot of courage," I told the wife, eyeing her ball bearings.

"Californians are kind of crazy," she admitted, "but it's a fun sport. You ought to try it."

"No, thanks. I like my feet, knees, and spine the way God designed them—intact."

Teen Son #2 had been sitting at the piano, attempting to play the Minute Waltz in fifty-three seconds (his latest hobby), and overheard our conversation. The next day he appeared outside after dinner, wearing a new pair of skates. His older brother and the grandfather next door quickly followed suit and joined our transplanted West Coast family in their nightly street rounds.

It wasn't long before the small group swelled to a crowd—more new skaters, but also three-year-old Colin from across the street, gleefully pedaling along on his Big Wheel, and Mr. Bates, a retiree who joined the gang via bicycle. "You know," I remarked to Mrs. California one night as she whisked by, executed a perfect left turn, and stopped two inches from me, "this is beginning to look like a parade."

She surveyed the group, chatting and gliding along on various sets of wheels. Someone was now riding a scooter. "You're right. Why don't we enter Hickory Avenue in the Fourth of July parade?"

I stared at her. Although our local Memorial Day parade was an annual extravaganza, boasting marching bands, veterans' groups, Scout units, and animal acts, the Fourth of July parade was just the opposite. By that time, school bands had been dismissed, half the population was away on vacation, and those that remained were treated to a dispirited line of fire engines, one depressed-looking juggler, and a few kazoo players. Only a carnival and fireworks saved the day from terminal lackluster. Mrs. California just didn't understand the situation.

"What would we *do* in the parade?" I asked.

"Do?" she waved an arm at the group, now hauling a fallen skater to her feet. "Just wear red, white, and blue, get on our bikes and skates—and go!"

"Sounds great," agreed another neighbor as tricycles skidded around us. "And we can have a block party afterward. Besides— who'll see us? No one ever comes to the Fourth of July parade."

Put like that, everyone agreed the idea had merit. The block party would bring neighbors out of their houses on a day meant for socializing. And although our group would do little to rival the kazoo players for excitement, at least the two-mile parade route would provide a change of scene and a little exercise.

We spread the word via printed bulletins, and the neighbors were cheerfully enthused about the *party*. Within days, people had donated picnic tables, barbeques, and toddler wading pools, and some even organized the food. But most drew the line at parade participation. "Are you kidding? Me, march with a bunch of kiddy cars and over-the-hill bikers?"

Even the parade partakers were lethargic at first. "Should I decorate my bike, Dad?" one middle schooler asked.

"If you like," her father shrugged. "There's some purple crepe paper in the attic."

"What about recorded music?" someone wondered.

"Too complicated," was the yawned consensus. "Let's just hum some John Philip Sousa."

The worm began to turn, however, when the five teenagers next door appeared on the street one evening dressed as a five-part living American flag. "We forgot we had it," one explained. He must have finally cleaned under his bed.

"Wow! Classy!" was the general reaction.

The worm turned more quickly when Mr. Bates fitted each parade bike with a handmade animal head from his wood shop (we hadn't decided on a theme, but animals seemed as reasonable as anything) and some Girl Scouts designed a banner to lead the group.

The worm positively spun, however, when the down-the-street music store proprietor appeared at my door. "I've got some advertising T-shirts I can't use," he explained. "The supplier stenciled the store name on the back instead of the front. Maybe you'd all like to wear them in the parade and look alike? It's a good way to keep track of the little kids too."

"I'm going as Sister Mary Hickory," I told him, "and my job is to keep the little ones safe and together. But the shirts—are they red, white, and blue?"

"Beige. But I could stencil "I'm a Hickory Nut" on the fronts in red. For free."

It was an offer we couldn't refuse, Mrs. California said, and everyone agreed. Those not marching could wear shirts and cheer from the sidelines. They might be the only audience there. We ordered two hundred.

On the morning of the Fourth, we met and headed over to the assembly. We were a weird-looking assortment with our beige "Lou's Music Shop—I'm a Hickory Nut" T-shirts, bicycles (some decorated, some not), baby buggies and wagons, wobbly skaters, several skateboarders who had joined at the last minute, and some senior citizens riding in a van decorated as an unidentified animal, paper eyelashes decking its headlights. (I, of course, was wearing a nun's habit, and aside from a few startled screams when they saw me, the kids were properly behaved.) Besides, who'd watch us?

"Something's odd," Mrs. California observed as she skated back from reconnoitering the assembly grounds. "Our number is sixty-seven. Could there be *that* many units in the parade?"

"Of course not," I started to say, and then as we rounded the corner, my mouth dropped. Marching bands in sleek uniforms, floats, drill teams, carloads of dignitaries, even a contingent of high-stepping horses . . . We had been too busy learning to skate to read the papers, too rushed to hear that the parade committee, tired of the usual dismal display, had arranged the greatest show on earth, one that thousands were lining up to view.

"We can't possibly . . ." We stared at each other, appalled. What if people laughed and ridiculed? What if they couldn't see what had been taking place on our block? But the bands began to play, and suddenly we remembered why we were really there. Humming "Stars and Stripes Forever," we moved out before a sea of grinning faces . . .

The best part, we all agreed that afternoon at the block party, had come when the judges had announced the winning unit. "To the Hickory Nuts," our trophy read, "for best personifying the American Neighborhood experience."

"We didn't even know there was a judging," I marveled as the trophy passed from one to another. "And to think it all started with a pair of skates."

"No," Mrs. California slipped an arm around me. "It all started with freedom, and with being an American."

"Happy Fourth," someone said. And we reached for the hot dogs.

You have to love a nation that celebrates its independence every July 4, not with a parade of guns, tanks, and soldiers who file by the White House in a show of strength and muscle, but with family picnics where kids throw Frisbees, the potato salad gets iffy, and the flies die from happiness. You may think you have overeaten, but it is patriotism.

—Erma Bombeck

Mother Doesn't Work

J was born in the era when the term "career change" usually meant leaving one's admin assistant job to get married. "Getting married" had its own definition: steeping oneself in domesticity and making endless payments on a sewing machine so one could whip up pajamas and curtains at the drop of a needle.

I tried to live up to the demands of my career. I waxed my driveway every Friday, kept a coupon file, and regularly polished the insides of the wastebaskets.

Then society changed. Pressing my nose against a spotless windowpane, I watched my contemporaries dashing off to real-estate classes or computer terminals while I stayed home regrouting the bathroom tile.

I was in a rut. But what was a woman to do when she'd spent years learning the rules of the game only to discover that the game was no longer being played?

"The first step on your road to rehab is called 'getting out of the house,'" announced my pal Lynne, who used our kitchen as a pit stop on her daily five-mile jogging route. "How about going to a movie with me tonight?"

"A movie?" I stopped polishing the oven lightbulb to consider it.

"They're in color now," Lynne prodded. "In fact, you can even bring a movie home and play it on your television set."

"Really?" It sounded unbelievable. "I wonder if the world is passing me by . . ."

"Duh. You'd be amazed at the way things have changed since our college days." Lynne watched me dust the pipes under the sink for a full minute before grabbing the cloth and flinging it out the window. "TV dinners, lip gloss, disposable diapers, automatic transmissions . . . Honestly, you've got to get with it before you collapse from terminal boredom."

"Okay." I took the plunge. "I'm in your hands."

Relieved, Lynne introduced me to the Great Outdoors, an area I noticed only when driving the high schoolers back and forth each hour to practices, study halls, and meals. Rehabilitating myself was fun. I made new friends—people who didn't call me Mommy and could cut their own meat. I'd roll out of bed each morning and feel my brain clicking to "On" as I wondered what exciting events this new day would bring. I guess it was inevitable that the next step would be "looking for a job."

Yes, it happens to just about all of us. The woman in her fifties who's never worked a day in her life (unless you count twenty or thirty years of sixteen-hour-a-day home front shifts) suddenly finds herself sneaking a peek at the classifieds, "just to see what's out there" (or perhaps to avoid babysitting the grandkids). Her younger counterpart, having combined grad school, a stint in the peace corps, and pregnancy, now feels the push to utilize all that education again.

And then there are people like me, somewhere in the middle. Our paychecks ended years ago when we entered the world of full-time motherhood. Dutifully, we logged volunteer time, perhaps picked up sporadic cash with a series of odd jobs, and had lots of fun along the way. But now something has changed. College bills loom, the youngest is finally in school, orthodontia or fallen arch surgery estimates have arrived, the living room furniture has collapsed—whatever the catalyst, we're faced with the need for additional loot. And for some of us, the need to respond to a growing restlessness that can no longer be ignored.

It must be great to be paid for one's labor, and I've heard that a job does wonders for a woman's psyche too—meeting other women in a competitive situation sometimes inspires a housewife to shed the extra pounds she's been carrying around since Baby #2 or retire her collection of ragged sweatshirts in favor of a more put-together look,

Getting hired to do something at regular intervals on an unyielding schedule also makes an efficiency expert out of many a ditz. One of my best friends was so disorganized that she spent her entire day going back and forth to the supermarket because she could only remember one item at a time. But when she finally returned to surgical nursing, she became a whirling dervish, completing all household chores and errands by six a.m. in order to be in her whites by seven. (Once she accidentally set her kids out with the garbage, but we've all done that, working or non-).

First, of course, we must send a trial balloon floating in front of our husbands. "I'm thinking about getting a job," I announced one evening after Spouse had dined royally on steak and chocolate pudding.

"You *have* a job." He lowered the sports page slightly. "Taking care of me, the children, and the house. There ought to be enough joy in that for any woman."

"My cup does run over," I assured him, resisting the urge to heave a large object in his direction. "But all of our kids are planning to attend Harvard. And did I show you the washing machine repair estimate? The fact is, I ought to be earning some money."

"You do earn money," he protested. (The newspaper, I noticed, was now on his lap.) "You write and you lecture, and sometimes you teach a course . . ."

"All sporadic and speculative," I explained. "What I need is a regular paycheck, something I can count on."

"But you have a regular paycheck *now!*" His newspaper was on the floor.

"I do?"

"Yes. Mine."

"Let's talk about it later," I soothed. "I think there's a bowl of chocolate pudding left."

My next step was a perusal of the want ads. I found I was eminently well qualified for the positions of short order cook, maid, prison guard, school bus driver, and nursery helper. The listing I was looking for, however—"Wanted: Talented homemaker to run small corporation. No experience necessary, childcare provided, name your salary and working hours"—never appeared. Instead I finally answered an ad for a public information coordinator. I reasoned that in my role as wife and mother I was expected to know absolutely everything, so this position ought to be right up my alley. Instead, it was a shattering experience.

Along with the other forty-eight applicants, I was handed a card to fill out, listing my previous work history. While the others scribbled merrily, I chewed the pencil, wondering if "scrubbing floors, polishing furniture, housebreaking a large spaniel" would qualify. Then there was the matter of character references. My pediatrician could probably testify to my fortitude under adverse conditions (if he recalled last spring's stomach flu epidemic), and my pastor would surely admit that I was outspoken at school board meetings ("outspoken" might be putting it rather charitably, but he is a charitable man). But were these the sort of résumé qualifications that would wow an employer?

Finally, it was my turn to enter the inner sanctum, where I discovered that the public information coordinator actually tossed together a four-page monthly newsletter and sent out press releases whenever there was something to say. "Why, what a relief," I told the interviewer. "I've been doing that sort of work for years, but we always called it volunteer publicity chairperson. Imagine that!"

"This position calls for a BA in journalism," he informed me loftily.

"I never finished college," I admitted, "but I've been a published writer for the past—"

"And approximately twelve hours a week . . ."

"Twelve hours! For a dinky little newsletter like that? I could do it in half the time—housewives learn to work *fast*, you know."

"And attendance at several seminars each year to learn the art of writing the press release . . ."

I laughed. "Believe me, there's no art to writing a press release. But I *have* heard of those time-wasting meetings where everyone sings Kumbaya . . ."

* * *

"I didn't get the job." I dragged myself home later and collapsed on Husband's shoulder.

"You were obviously overqualified and way too honest," he patted my head. "Haven't I told you not to cast your pearls before swine? Besides, we need you here more than the business world does." The relief on his face was obvious.

My foray into the outside world could have ended there. But sometime later, I happened to meet a local typesetter who didn't care a fig about my university connections, character, or pizza preference. "Are you a reliable proofreader and editor?" he wanted to know. "And can you have the work back on time?"

I could and did—until I quit to write books about angels. And that's another story.

But the typesetter job taught me that finding good work is less a matter of talent and credentials and more a matter of dogged persistence. And a belief in the abilities we've developed as housewives. And overcoming our intimidation. And expecting to do the best job we can. And making lots and lots of chocolate pudding.

Chance can allow you to accomplish a goal every once in a while, but consistent achievement happens only if you love what you are doing.

—*Bart Conner*

The Way My Kids Live with Me

Husband and I have recently realized that we will one day be planning our retirement. He has labeled a drawer "Places to go someday." The Ozarks Chamber of Commerce sent a delightful catalogue, and so did an obscure community in Michigan's Upper Peninsula (although I have no intention of visiting, much less living, anywhere snow can possibly fall). Then he began seriously thinking about what sort of hobbies he will pursue once he has an abundance of leisure time. Since his current hobbies are napping and answering the phone, this should be interesting. I have suggested pursuits for him such as weeding, drying dishes, and becoming acquainted with detergents; I figure he'll need to know these things when I'm off on my sabbaticals because, contrary to my better half's intentions, my retirement plans involve living with my children. Each of them, one at a time, will host me for a fun-filled month or two every year.

I'm making a list of the things I'll pack and the activities I'll pursue once I get to each house, and it looks like my sunset years will be quite fulfilling. I can hardly wait to live with the kids the way they live with me.

I'm going to pack a guitar with an electric amplifier—I've

always wanted to learn how to play one—and will schedule practice for one or two a.m. when there's adequate time to really concentrate. I'll bring along nine tubes of shampoo, all with missing caps, a hundred empty pop cans to roll under my bed, and marbles to scatter along hallways and stairs, wherever people are apt to walk barefoot in the dark. I'll keep string, notes from my friends, crackers, rubber bands, tennis balls, fish food, dice, playing cards, and magazines in my bureau drawers. And I'll put my clean underwear under my bed. My door will bear a handmade welcome sign: "Stay Out! This Means You, Jerk!" I'm sure they'll understand.

When my lawyer son entertains his clients or partners at dinner, I'll be the perfect guest. I'll come to the table in baggy pants, tap my teaspoon impatiently against my nose, complain loudly about the menu ("filet mignon again?"), upset my milk, argue with (and eventually punch) the man sitting next to me, fall off my chair at least once, and whine that the woman across the table got a bigger piece of dessert than I did.

I'll get up very early because I'll have lots of things to do. I'll have a paper route, of course—one that is located many blocks away, one that involves snow, rain, and hurricanes. Since the papers must be delivered before six a.m., especially on Sundays, everyone in the family will naturally get up to help. (I, of course, keep all the money. Heaven only knows what kind of a pittance my social security check will be by then, and of course each child will help to fund me.)

I also intend to try out for cheerleading, a part in the local play, and a spot in the community band—all things I never had time to do when I was raising them. Since I won't have a car, my offspring will be assigned chauffeur duty, picking me up at midnight or, better still, whenever I call. When I do drive their cars,

I'll make sure the gas gauge is left on E.

The remainder of my waking hours will no doubt be spent pounding on the bathroom door yelling, "Get out! It's my turn!" I'll put an empty ice cube tray back in the freezer and make constant phone calls, even dialing Time and Temperature in Moscow or Rome. (When my child has the nerve to be on the phone, I'll stand on her shoes, whimper for a cookie, or fight loudly with my grandchildren.) Of course I'll scatter popcorn, paper, sweaters, bath powder, overdue library books, and muddy shoes around the house to give it that lived-in look.

It will be fun watching television with my offspring too. I'll insist on a steady diet of cartoons and rock videos—newscasts, animal documentaries, ball games, and Masterpiece Theatre will be strictly off limits. No one will be permitted to talk to me except during commercials, and even then my side of the dialogue will be limited to "Huh?," "Can I have some pop?," "It's her turn," and "Stop looking at me!"

Shopping trips will be delightful. I'll dash up and down the supermarket aisles, knocking down displays and shrieking, "I want a quarter for the gumball machine!" Everyone in the store will stare at my child, who will attempt to placate me by buying me a candy bar. The candy will have nuts, so I'll throw it away and fling myself on the floor, kicking and screaming, "I hate you! You're mean!"

If we survive the supermarket, we'll visit the mall, where I'll get lost three times, peek under dressing-room doors, and play hide-and-seek with another retiree in a display window. My child will decide to put off shopping until I move on to her brother's house and will, no doubt, graciously buy me a train ticket that very day. But I won't be able to leave just then because I'll still have to throw a tantrum during the pastor's homily at church; trample through a just-seeded garden; break a neighbor's window; ask my child loudly in a crowded elevator where babies come from; hide all flashlights, scissors, and cell phones under the couch; and draw on walls that have just been painted.

My husband doesn't think I'll have the nerve. But actually, I can't wait. Retirement is going to be so much fun!

Very few people in the past would have liked living with their parents beyond childhood. In fact, many people did not like living with their parents during their childhood.

—*Dennis Prager*

What You
Don't Know . . .

It was the first week in August—National Smile Week—and I was definitely wearing one as I entered a major department store to buy a pair of white sandals for our upcoming vacation at Lake Kitchiegumba. Admittedly Lake K is ten years behind in fashion trends, so my offspring refuse to be seen with me if what I'm wearing threatens to ruin their social lives. I was thinking over the possibility of leaving them behind this year when . . .

. . . Inside the store I looked around, blinked, went outside to check the mall calendar, determined that, yes, it still was August (to say nothing of National Smile Week), and reentered the store. Angora gloves, black wool suits, reindeer ski pants—oh, and plastic pumpkins next to the stacks of ceramic turkey platters.

When would I learn? Once again I had forgotten the merchandiser code: people silly enough to look for sandals in August or parkas in February shall have their credit cards temporarily impounded until the next twenty-percent-off-remaining-stock sale.

It's perplexing. Don't store owners and buyers understand that folks who have yet to lose their Christmas poundage (and need to work up to three-way mirrors on a gradual basis) are psychologically unable to shop for bathing suits in January when those size-four customers deem it prudent to display them? Can't they appreciate the fact that I can't face thick beige turtlenecks in the middle of the sundress season? The retailer who comes up with the incredibly brilliant idea of selling fly swatters and sleds when people actually want them will make a major killing. But I suppose we shouldn't hold our breath. "Experts" seem to have a backward Alice-in-Wonderland approach to everything in life.

I can't be the only gullible one who got caught in the great oat bran caper some years back. There I was, carefully measuring my daily intake and feeling both virtuous and up-to-date, when suddenly the same researchers reversed course and determined that oat bran was worthless in terms of lowering cholesterol, and only slightly better than mayonnaise sandwiches on the overall good-health scale. Talk about betrayal! The very next week I, the first person in the neighborhood to travel the decaffeinated coffee route, discovered that it actually *raises* that tricky cholesterol, and that's not good for the heart. Neither is high blood pressure—and mine is going higher with each passing fad.

There's no sure thing. What if we discover that other sacrifices we're making in the interest of increased stamina and trim waistlines are also unnecessary—or even harmful? Will salads someday be named as a source of itchy ear lobes? What if eating excess grain causes double vision or cracks in one's teeth? How about fluoride in our drinking water? Will some lab technician determine that it leads to hardening of the tonsils or midriff bulge? Will yogurt prove to be detrimental to creaking joints, and wok recipes radioactive? What if raw carrots are responsible for bad dreams or global warming and cooling?

It's not that I applaud ignorance, but knowing too much can be as hazardous to one's health as not knowing enough. After being bombarded day and night by media experts about the seven warning signs of cancer, the five danger signals for gallstones, or the three indications that I might be coming down with dandruff, I'm certainly confused (one of the six steps to mononucleosis) and having a hard time falling asleep (which is a forecast, I think, of either low blood pressure or gout). Between watching for preservatives, worrying about impending gall bladder disease, and trying to decide what to pack for our week at Lake Kitchiegumba, it's no wonder I'm coming down with low blood sugar and an allergy to making plans.

"Thank heavens it's time for a vacation," I told Husband when I returned from my futile shopping trip. "If I stay inside all week (to avoid contaminated salmon); rest; drink plenty of bottled water; refuse to fold, spindle, or mutilate; and don't read any newspapers, I'll probably avoid hearing about the latest additive that researchers once thought was safe but have now determined causes split ends."

Husband lowered the editorial page. "What are you talking about?" he asked. "Weren't we planning to take a few quiet walks around Lake Kitchiegumba, just the two of us, so we could finish our sentences?"

"What if we run into diseased mosquitoes?" I challenged him, "or stop at a hot dog stand that uses filler instead of corn-fed cattle for meat? What if the kids are unsupervised for more than a second or two and use the wrong brand of sun block? No wait—didn't some doctor decide that we're using too much sunblock and not getting enough Vitamin D . . . ?"

"We'll survive. And speaking of sun, I think it's frying your brain," Husband soothed in his usual understanding manner. "I tell you what: I'll take you on a shopping spree in town this year. You can buy some white sandals—the ones you've got are looking kind of grim, don't you think?

"Great idea," I assured him. "Our very own treasure hunt."

"Huh?"

"Never mind." Why should I spoil the surprise? After all, it's National Smile Week.

For years, my husband and I have advocated separate vacations. But the kids keep finding us.

—Erma Bombeck

Summer's End

Well, Lord, it's over. Did I think I'd survive, even with your ever-present help, occasional tantrums (mine), and a dose or two of guilt therapy? Honestly, no, but despite my foreboding, my brood has just piled out the back door looking cleaner than they have all summer. It's the first day of school.

Yes, I know that my hand is shaking slightly as I pour a cup of coffee—I have not yet become accustomed to the morning rush.

"Puffed Fruities in the orange bowl, orange juice in the yellow cup, please . . ."

"I'm not really hungry, Ma. Can I have a half dozen eggs over easy and a turkey sandwich to tide me over till lunch?"

"Mother-r-r, somebody's taken my math book! I left it right here on the dining room table last month . . ."

"Hon, how come you're so crabby in the morning? You should go to bed earlier."

Forgive me, Father, for my summer failings. For the times I grumbled over underbed debris, the ever-present array of dirty glasses filling the sink, and the small fries (some I'd never met) waiting to be bathed. Did the kids know that, at times, I secretly resented their loud and constant presence? How awful if they did, for they are my heart's desire, despite that time when Teen ate the six pounds of ground beef I was saving for the evening barbeque. "Just to tide me over until the baseball game, Ma; I didn't know someone else had dibs."

Did the kids realize I was sometimes envious of their freedom, furtively resentful of other families jetting off to exciting vacation spas? Even though I am your saintly daughter, Lord, I do have trouble with the "Why me?"—or in the case of wealthy pals, "Why not me?"—syndrome. That's okay for me, but not okay if the gang suspected.

Forgive me for the plans that never materialized because "Mom's got a deadline today," the family prayers that went unsaid because "it's just too hot." In summer, time seems looming just ahead when I'll do all the things I've "temporarily" set aside. I should have learned by now that the perfect someday never comes, and "carpe diem" should be everyone's motto.

And yet, Lord, as always, you sent blessings. Cool lemonade in late afternoon, more pleasant because a neighbor (stopping by to borrow my egg beater) shared it. A garden that yielded not only flowers but vegetables, the taste of summer all winter long. "Okra seeds are never bargains if no one eats okra," Husband explains to budding gardener, what we in the parent business call a "teachable moment." Sunsets heralding the close of satisfying days. ("How come he gets to stay up later than me, Mom? Huh, Mom? Huh?")

There were gifts for my spirit too, Father—gifts that only your summer can bestow. Teens coming home from part-time jobs, tanned and tired, yet wearing the unmistakable aura of emerging adulthood. "Mrs. Parr plays her game from the neighboring fairway," Teen laughs, "but she bought me four hot dogs to tide me over till the eighteenth hole. She's really a nice lady." Unexpected guests and the joy of friendship long savored.

Now summer has once again slipped away, and I am left in the stillness of my kitchen. I will relish the coming winter silence, Lord, the chance to complete a project, think a coherent thought. But summer's waning brings the bittersweet awareness of the passage of time, the realization that things will never again be the same. A child goes off to college this year, a wedding looms just ahead; time and its relentless march waits for no one.

Help me make the most of each new day, Lord. Whatever the season, let me be grateful for your gift of life, your ever-present love, your forgiveness when I fail to honor you—and the family you gave me. Teach me to savor your daily blessings, the beauty to be found in each passing moment as it brings me—all of us— closer to eternity with you.

Father, thank you once again for summer.

A life without love is like a year without summer.

—Swedish Proverb

Who's She?

I *have written* about the Hickory Nuts, a group of families living on Hickory Avenue. During those golden years, we wore lettered T-shirts ("I'm a Hickory Nut"), marched in the Fourth of July parade (always winning a trophy), and hosted several get-togethers during the year as a contribution to neighborliness. We Nuts cared for each other in many ways, watching each other's children, lending tools and recipes, turning out full strength for baptisms and tree trimmings. But one of the most memorable events occurred shortly after my first book about angels was published.

I had written six earlier books about varying subjects—not all that exciting as the sales figures eventually indicated. For some odd reason, my new publisher decided the angel book was worthy of a little more promotion than merely printing up some announcement postcards for me to send to my distant relatives. First they sent me to a few cities to give speeches about the book. The last time I had been on a plane was when I took my then-toddler for a visit to my sister and disgraced myself by clutching the arm of the stranger sitting next to me and sobbing.

"You can level with me. We're going to die, aren't we?" I wept, and he responded calmly, "I don't think so. We haven't left the ground yet."

However, the publisher wasn't aware of my phobia, and I managed to keep it hidden until it actually went away. The publishers then arranged some speeches for me. You will recall that in my earlier book, *Moms Go Where Angels Fear to Tread*, I explained how my fear of standing up in front of people went away too. And no one at home seemed to notice my absence, so this was an unexpected bonus.

Then came a downer. The publishers arranged with a local store to host a book signing for me. My only job, it appeared, was to alert my public to turn out for the occasion.

There was just one problem. I didn't have a public.

Oh, local people knew I was a writer, but it was usually heralded with the same degree of fascination as someone who raises guinea hens or processes insurance forms: "That's nice. What else is new?" This suited me fine and led to an anonymity that I cherished. (Who wants to wonder how her hair looks when she's just running into the store to buy cheese?) But now I was expected to somehow pull an adoring crowd to the shopping mall.

Even worse was the public nature of the project. See, when I do a radio show interview, I don't know for sure that no one's listening. When I publish a magazine article, I don't know for sure that no one is reading it. But an autograph party brings one face-to-face with the reality that *no one is buying my book*. It can be a humbling experience, as if I needed another.

This wasn't my first signing. No, on that memorable day a few years ago, a lady had gone by the table (where I sat alone, praying silently that this torture would soon end), then stopped and looked back at me (I smiled tentatively), then started on her way again—then stopped, turned, and headed straight for me. "Tell me," she said as she leaned across the table, "Are you . . . Somebody?"

I had been reaching for a book to sign for her, and her question took me by surprise. "Well . . ." I hesitated. "No, not really."

"I didn't think so!" she announced triumphantly and continued her walk. A couple of potential buyers, having heard my confession, followed her like lemmings.

During other events, fellow authors and I had shared our embarrassing moments: a store staff that didn't know there was a book signing today and thus couldn't direct customers to the table; the table itself hidden behind a giant plant or pole or far too close to the ice-cracking machine; only four books in stock; screaming toddlers running by while Writer attempts to give a casual speech to three people who sat down to rest their feet . . . But of course the worst scenario possible was the dreaded event-that-no-one-attended. This situation, everyone agreed, was always the author's fault. Obviously she had no following, and the store management would think long and hard about ever welcoming her back.

And so, the week before the signing, I took courage in hand and wrote a note to the Nuts. "I hate book signings," I told them. "You sit there, surrounded by piles of unsold books, while shoppers go by, asking each other, "Who's that, Ethel?" and Ethel responds, "Search me—I've never heard of her.

"So I'm throwing myself on your mercy. Do you have a special friend who might like a book as a gift? (You could read it first.) If not, could you come anyway so I won't feel so alone? If you can't come, would you send your kids? Would you send your dogs?"

My daughter dropped copies in everyone's mailbox while I made up a list of potential customers. I'd call the newspaper editor, make an announcement at the church's Pot Luck Supper, notify the bridge club, tell the regulars at morning Mass, call in markers from any woman whose carpool I ever drove . . . People in my prayer group had mentioned lately the possibility of starting a Hovering Ministry for me; members who appear at signings and float around the table as if they were interested, thereby attracting some real customers. But nothing had been arranged as yet.

Then disaster struck me, in the form of the flu bug and a sore throat, and out the window my plans went. No telephone calls. No announcements. Just chicken soup and tissue boxes and depression.

"You'll be all right by the signing," my husband reassured me as he peered at the thermometer.

"What signing?" I croaked miserably. "No one knows about it except the Hickory Nuts, and you know how busy this neighborhood is on Saturdays. No one will come. I'll be ruined . . ."

"I'll call your mother," Spouse suggested. "She's always good for a few copies."

"Will *you* come?" I wheezed desperately.

He looked uncertain. "I'd really love to, but I was planning to hose down the driveway on Saturday." I burst into tears.

I was feeling better by Saturday, however—just well enough to meet my doom. I considered driving off the road into a ditch, thus canceling the event, but my shoes were new and the ditch was muddy and my will needed updating. (Who would I leave all those unsold books to?)

And the publisher and store personnel had done an amazingly nice job. The table was set up out in the mall, in front of the store. Copies of my book smiled happily from a window display, and a large photo of me was hanging above the table. (Shoppers were already looking at it and asking, "Who's she?") I felt terribly guilty as I slipped into a chair, half hidden by the stacks. All this for nothing.

Well, at least my mother and dad, always loyal, were there. "We happened to be in the neighborhood," Mom explained comfortably. "And your cousin Donna is coming too, if she gets her cast removed in time." (Good hovering—Donna has nine children. My spirits rose slightly.)

"Look," Dad pointed. "Isn't that a Hickory Nut?"

It was—the young nurse from next door, and her mother. "Your note brought tears to my eyes," nurse Kate told me. "We figured the least we could do would be to come and hang around."

"Hi, Ginny!" Kate's mother was waving at another Nut—no, two—who were making their way toward the table.

"We came to be with you in your hour of need," Ginny told me. "I'll take three books. So what's new, Connie?"

Connie, who had just donated blood and had several kids in tow, took off her coat. "We couldn't let Joan go through this ordeal alone," she explained briskly to a crowd of shoppers that was slowly gathering around the table. "Grab some books, kids, before they're all gone. Isn't this fun?"

"Look, there's Kathie," someone announced. "She *did* bring her dog!"

"Can I have your autograph?" a small boy asked shyly. I looked around to see who he was talking to. It was me.

"Can I buy a book?" asked a stranger.

"My gosh, look!" someone shouted from the end of the mall. "Jim, is that . . . could it be . . . why, that's *Joan Wester Anderson*!" It was the California couple doing a scene deserving of an Academy Award. But it worked. As they ran toward my table, screaming and excited, shoppers from other parts of the mall hurried toward our growing crowd, not wanting to miss anything. And no one asked, "Who?" (The Californians ended up reenacting this scene every fifteen minutes or so, just long enough to clear out one group of hoverers and welcome another.)

I don't remember how many books we sold that day. But I do remember feeling warm, cared for, and once again grateful for the friendship and support of a very special group.

Thanks, Hickory Nuts. I love you.

My friends are my estate.

—*Emily Dickinson*

Clothes Encounters

*O*ur *best* friends buried a thirty-pound bag of silver coins in their garden. My neighbor prefers flipping houses. And my bridge partner swears by the Dow. Husband and I, however, have taken a different route to retirement riches. We've invested in fabrics futures.

While other people's treasures nestle tidily in sacks or safety deposit boxes, ours require an entire floor. The attic is filled—nay, *stuffed* to the rafters—with our outdated clothes. Committed to the adage that what goes around comes around, we believe that it's only a matter of time before my middy blouse and his white bucks will be back in style. And why spend our hard-earned cash on new models when we have perfectly decent leftovers stashed for the occasion? We might even open a resale shop, stocked with our faded collection, and clean up on this most common of markets. The possibilities are endless.

Oh, we realize we are taking our chances. Frankly, I can't recall my mother's three-piece bathing suit ever making a comeback, nor has there been much of a demand lately for the bustle or stovepipe hat. Even my favorite T-shirt—JESUS LOVES YOU (But I'm His Favorite)—is getting a little ratty around the edges. But Husband and I are an adventuresome pair, and temporarily tolerating a top-heavy house seems a small price to pay to be first with the latest—someday.

There is a problem, however. The attic is definitely becoming a fire hazard, so periodically we wedge ourselves into a space between the garment bags and discuss a new disposal plan. "I have an idea," Husband told me recently. "Remember how I overcame my addiction to cigarettes?"

"Sure. You switched to cigars."

"No. I gave them up little by little. Couldn't we try that—say, bring *just* the Bermuda shorts to the Goodwill collection box?"

I paled. "Then we'd have to sacrifice all those knee socks and suspenders too, or nothing would match!"

"Well, we can't save everything!" He glanced around for inspiration.

"Okay." I reached for his high school warm-up jacket, the one that's missing a sleeve. "Let's toss this relic."

"Don't be ridiculous—that's a collector's item. How about getting rid of these rags of yours?" he asked, holding up my wedding dress and veil.

In more lucid moments, we also wonder if the clothes will ever fit us again (besides our family, other things have doubled in the past few decades.) Perhaps it is impractical for a woman immersed in a midlife crisis to hang onto a pink net prom dress. And would I really want to wear that white felt poodle skirt again? But somehow I know that the moment I dispose of those penny loafers, or Husband pitches his yellow polyester leisure suit, the designers will declare them the "in" things. And won't we feel silly then?

Of course, with so much attic finery waiting to be resurrected and resold, I feel guilty buying anything new, so my current wardrobe, consisting of two good suits and a pair of jeans, rests in a small drawer. Which makes life difficult for our teen daughter since she has little to borrow. "Yuck," she muttered yesterday, peering into my closet. "When are you going to get a new outfit?"

"When are *you*?" I countered. "You spent your entire first semester clothing allowance on a fake fur coat and three pairs of underpants . . ."

"It's been a long school year," she admitted. "What I really need now is some pointy-toed skinny heels for work, some miniskirts . . ."

"Pointy-toed shoes? Minis? Are they back in style?"

Daughter shot me a withering glance. "Mom, this is the twenty-first century."

"Maybe," I murmured, "and maybe not. Let's take a tour of the attic."

Husband heard her delighted squeals from the curb that evening as he pulled into the driveway. "She's been up there all day," I told him.

"Finding a costume for a party?"

"No, refurbishing her wardrobe. She calls it 'vintage.' Did you know my maternity clothes look just like the overblouses everyone's wearing today? She even called the boys and told them about your plaid shoelace collection. They're on their way over."

Husband grinned. "Looks like our investment paid off."

"Not in the way we expected. But the kids are ecstatic, and maybe now we can buy ourselves some up-to-date duds."

"Good idea." He eyed my denim cutoffs and Chicago Cubs T-shirt. "And let's burn those while we're at it."

Not a chance. If I keep them packed away until the Cubs win the World Series, I'll be the envy of the whole neighborhood.

Every generation laughs at the old fashions, but follows, religiously, the new.

—*Henry David Thoreau*

Pet Peeves

*W*e *have* much in life to be grateful for. But at the risk of sounding less than gracious, I mention a few of my not-so-favorite recurring episodes. Blowing off steam is good for one's mental health, I've been told, so does anyone else take umbrage at

- Personnel in doctors' offices who shout at me from behind the glass reception cage after I've registered: "How old are you? You didn't fill that in! And what is your problem again?" Why do I have to report this from my across-the-room plastic chair while the rest of those in the waiting room stare avidly?

- Drivers who don't have correct change at toll booths but realize it only when they reach the basket, or the right-handed drivers who toss coins with their left hand and, of course, miss the basket completely?

- Since we're on the road, what about drivers who wait until the light turns green to put on their left turn signal? Or teen drivers who, in effect, steer giant boom boxes on wheels; you hear them coming in plenty of time to get out of their way (into the nearest ditch), but the music drowns out the sounds of train whistles, nuclear explosions, or other drivers beeping at you to tell you your seven-year-old is dangling his sister out the side window.

- Adolescent offspring who reprogram the station on my car radio when they borrow it, then leave a blast of rock to blow me out of my seat the next morning when I turn on the ignition. I'm especially peeved about this one.
- Static cling. Where does it come from? Why do we get it?
- People who understand odds. When a sports fan says a certain team is a nine-to-four favorite, I agree without any idea what he's talking about. Ditto about car parts. If the altimeter needs replacing or polishing, I attempt to look intelligent or even dismayed, but frankly, it's all Latin to me.
- Folks who make spectacles out of themselves when they scream at the umpire or, worse, at the child athlete. Admittedly, I and all the moms of daughters on the third-grade volleyball team were once ejected from a gym for unsportsmanlike behavior. We've since learned to curb the urge to scream, "Kill her!"
- People who phone you, then put you on hold. Does anyone have a polite way of solving this modern atrocity? Hanging up while the caller is handling another line seems rude. But hanging on—especially while Caller discusses possibilities with a driveway salesman—is something I'll do only for my nearest and dearest.
- Toy displays in grocery stores, especially near the check-out lines. Supermarket managers ought to be forced, as part of their training, to shop with a cartload of melting food, push or pull a second cart containing a two-year-old, and keep an eye on a four-year-old. Add their screams over the display of cartoon character dolls to the scenario, accompanied by the glares of other customers who view the havoc with disdain.

- Waitresses who announce "My name is Esther Lou. I'll be your server tonight." Shouldn't we have figured that out since she's handing us the menus? I'm never sure if this practice calls for a response. Perhaps I should introduce myself to Esther Lou, and insist that she view the most recent photos of the kids.
- Door-to-door solicitors and the local Brownies who come selling wares when I'm in a bubble bath or in the middle of explaining to my child's preschool teacher that my child is not here at home, nor should he be and what do they mean that they've *lost track* . . .
- Telephone solicitors who begin by saying, "Hi! How are you tonight?" I'm extremely un-fine if I'm still trying to enjoy that bubble bath or find my preschooler.
- Electronic devices that cannot be reset after a power failure because there is no specific button marked "On." DVDs designed so poorly that technologically impaired parents can't operate them and must beg for assistance from their children who are away at camp: "Just punch the button marked 'Power,' Mom, then click on 'Pre-record,' and then . . ."
- Low-cal popcorn. What's the point?
- Lists like these. They always make me feel so grumpy.

Thanks, God, for reminding me that if I have nothing more to complain about than these silly entries, I am indeed a blessed woman.

The secret of happiness is to count your blessings while others are adding up their troubles.

—*Anonymous*

A Time to Mourn

It was a breathtakingly beautiful October Sunday, the kind of day where nothing bad could happen. My mother and I were chatting on the phone as she made lunch for my father, who was expected home any minute from ushering at church. But my father didn't appear at the front door. Instead, it was the pastor, and by the time he gave my mother the terrible news, I had already started to turn numb.

Our first major loss. None of us were able to grasp it. How could the day continue, people and traffic moving along in the sun, just as if our world hadn't abruptly ended? Yes, everyone dies, but usually there's some notice, a chance to say good-bye. As we gathered, half our tears were for the lack of warning, no final hugs or hand-holding. The other half was the dawning realization that something vital had gone out of our family. No matter how he had left us, without our father, his warm personality, his love freely given, even his unique imagination and fix-it foibles, life had forever changed. He would never meet five of his grandchildren—my brother's family had just begun—or play golf again with my sons or tinker with some strange unidentifiable pieces and—Voila!—make something unique out of them.

We had our faith, of course—a firm belief in the hereafter—and intellectually we knew we would see our father again. But head knowledge is not of the heart, nor does it comfort those afflicted by grief, at least not for a long time. Pain would be our companion; we would awaken in the mornings with the weight of it pressing us down—before we even identified the feeling—and we would go to bed with it at night, tossing and turning. *I do believe, help my unbelief* . . . "Does it ever go away?" I asked my husband, whose parents had already made their journey to heaven.

"It does," he reassured me. "But it takes time."

Time. Those first few days were like a fog. It was my husband's finest hour—getting groceries, arranging flights for the college kids, picking people up, consoling our immediate family. (Only later did I realize that he had sacrificed his own grieving, waiting until his wife and children were able to cope again.) It was my worst hour, as I told a nun, one of many who turned out for the wake. "Why," she patted me, "your father's closer to you now than he's ever been."

Yes, but how do I know that for sure? I wanted to ask. What if the God we serve is not a loving Father after all? What if He judges with a harsh set of rules? Who could pass the test? Even my father, the most perfect person I had ever known, might have trouble living up to it all. And then what?

If my father wasn't in heaven, then I didn't want to go there either, God.

But I said nothing, ashamed at my own weakness. Faith is not a feeling, but a decision. And in everyone's life, there are times when doubt creeps in. During those moments, one walks in darkness, I realized, but keeps looking for the light. It is the only way.

Weeks passed, and the raw misery did not heal. But in some small ways, it seemed less intense. As the first Christmas without him passed, we heaved a collective sigh of relief. With our extended family and friends to support us, we had made it through. My brother took the chair at the head of the table, my mother continued to set a positive tone, and somehow it all seemed manageable.

Months passed. *A time for mourning and a time for dancing . . .* We picked up the familiar strands of life once again; we laughed; we even started to reminisce, probing as one does with a sore tooth. How much pain will accompany this memory? Can I share it? Can you? We noticed little clues, signs, events that seemed to be specifically Dad-related. Was it he, sending greetings, consolation from a heavenly realm?

Lent came, a time to focus once again on the difficult parts of life. But Jesus walked with us in a far more prominent position this year. And when the journey seemed to be too long, too sad, I remembered the "Footprints" prayer and gave thanks. On Easter morning, as the world around me rejoiced, the broken pieces of my heart seemed to be mending in a new and stronger way.

Another summer, this time without Dad puttering in our garage. But my thinking seemed to be a bit clearer now, and I was able to realize something overlooked during this past year: The mourning, the sorrow and grief had been about *us*—our doubts, our loss. It had never been about him. If we had been able to see things from his viewpoint, without our own pain intruding, we would have been joyful beyond measure. For from the moment he left, we all knew where he was going and that our family reunion would indeed transpire some wonderful day. Our pain had clouded things, but it was lifting, and life would be good again.

And then it was October, another golden day, just like the one that had changed us forever. There would be more losses; just as every family has beginnings, all have endings too. But I would rather have gone through this past year a thousand times than lived a life without my father in it. The price had been high, but it was well worth paying. Raking leaves in the backyard, I sensed his presence, his smile, and my spirit rose. "Good-bye, Dad," I whispered. "See you in eternity."

I have fought the good fight. I have completed the race. I have kept the faith.

—*2 Timothy 3:7*

Love, Joan (Again)

Dear Lynne,

I was delighted to receive your Christmas card, and it's good to hear that you and the family are settling happily under the Phoenix sun. Congratulations on your goal to streamline this year! You can see by the date that I'm a bit behind, as usual. Recently I took a look at my home office and wondered—if I died, who would ever come in here and try to sort this out? Husband, with a stack of plastic garbage bags? Was that fair, me romping through the hills of heaven, carefree and joyful, and someone here trying to find my password for Facebook or Twitter? I'm going to keep at it this time, I swear, at least until I discover what color my carpet actually is.

Yes, our new neighbors are nice, but they'll never take your place. I miss Sally too. That's the trouble with friendships; the minute you start to really love someone, she moves out of your life in some way. It's hard to believe that Sally's been gone for two years. She seems to be enjoying South Dakota, which is a surprise. I mean, I can't envision Sally on top of a horse or even a mountain—do they have mountains in South Dakota? I *can* picture her sitting on the porch of a log cabin embroidering "Welcome to our humble hearth" on a sampler. She always was domestic, wasn't she?

Got to run, Lynne. A policeman is at the door. Give my best to the family. There's no reason we can't stay in touch now that we all have email.

Love,
Joan

* * *

October 13

Dear Lynne,

Yes, yes, and yes! What a wonderful idea—the three of us getting together for a madcap weekend in some centrally located spot. How about Nassau? ☺ I don't think our husbands would mind playing hausfrau for one measly weekend, do you? Actually, though, there's no point in mentioning it to the guys yet; let's wait until we hear from Sally. January sounds fine to me. My creative welding class will be over by then.

Love,
Joan

* * *

October 16

Dear Sally,

Your active life sounds so . . . active. It's not every midwestern-born-and-bred housewife who can learn to rope cattle. Somehow I still picture you at the end of a knitting needle instead of a lariat.

Congratulations on the new baby. I wondered why we hadn't heard from you in a while! Yes, I understand why a January weekend would be impossible since you're taking the twins on a camping trip to Death Valley to celebrate their graduation from preschool. We'll try for February instead.

Love,
Joan

* * *

October 20

Dear Lynne,

Glad to hear that your sulks paid off, and Bob is definitely going along with our weekend getaway plans. Every woman deserves some time for herself. No, I haven't brought the matter up with Husband yet—I thought it would be prudent to wait until the dentist bill is paid before spending money on a plane ticket.

Have you given any thought to the location of our rendezvous? Paris and Rome do sound appealing, but I thought you were still afraid to fly longer than fifteen or twenty minutes.

Love,
Joan

* * *

October 26

Dear Sally,

Yes, we've settled on the last weekend in April. Lynn and I have jam-packed schedules till then. We're open to suggestions on locations. It's sweet of you to invite us to your house, but the purpose of this vacation, sweet Sally, is to get *away* from it all.

Lynne refuses to take a Greyhound bus all the way from Phoenix anyway, so it looks as if you and I will have to go west. I do wish she could get over this neurosis about flying objects. That one bad experience with the can opener has probably ruined her.

I haven't mentioned our plans to Spouse yet; I'm waiting for the estimate on the new furnace. I told you about our smoke damage, didn't I? If not, I'll save it for our get-together; you'll die laughing!

Love,
Joan

* * *

October 30

Dear Lynne,

Frankly, Omaha isn't my idea of a scenic spot either, but the important thing is just to get together, even if we have to meet in some train station, don't you think?

* * *

November 1

Dear Lynne,

No, I wasn't serious about meeting in a train station. But Sally is a bit miffed that we turned down her suggestion to back-pack in the Rockies. Would you make sure she's on board for Omaha?

* * *

November 3

Dear Sally,

Congratulations on being elected Regional Hoedown Queen. It must be quite an honor. I can certainly understand why you would want to appear at the state square dancing marathon, but does it have to be the last weekend in April? I'll ask Lynne if we can push our plans back a weekend or two; my sprained elbow should be doing better by then. I did tell you about that, didn't I?

Love,
Joan

* * *

November 15

Dear Lynne,

Great to hear that your in-laws are returning next week for an indefinite stay. Your new job sounds exciting too, although I am surprised that you have gone back to work so soon after quitting. I realize that your schedule is going to be even more crowded, but couldn't you make time for one weekend? After all, this whole thing was *your* idea.

Love,
Joan

* * *

November 15

Dear Sally,

Yes, I'm disappointed about our plans falling through, and so is Lynne. But the trip has only been postponed, not abandoned.

Of course Husband was enthusiastic about it. He'd been sleeping in the garage just to gain a little privacy. You know these men and their midlife crises.

Remember that morning when we discussed what friendship really means? Lynne said that a friend was someone who could hear the meaning hidden behind the words. You thought that a friend was someone you could ask to go home. I had paraphrased Aristotle: "A friend is one soul in two bodies." In our case, three bodies.

There'll be other chances to meet. We loved each other enough to make the attempt, and that's what's important. Take care. Keep in touch. And congratulations on your morning sickness.

Love,
Joan

A friend is a gift you give yourself.

—*Robert Louis Stevenson*

Class Dismissed

November is famous for many things, but the most significant for families who have a college freshman is the child's first reentry to the home front since we deposited him or her on campus, and tried to refrain from cheering at the thought that we weren't losing a child, but regaining custody of the car.

It's important to understand that your collegiate has made some landmark adjustments during these past few months. She's learned to share a dorm refrigerator with forty-five other people, to eat on fifty cents a week, and (surprise) that a pile of soggy sweatclothes lying on the floor may, in time, grow fur. (Under no circumstances will it automatically convert into freshly laundered stacks.)

Given these shocks, Frosh needs downtime to reacclimate—and so do you. For one thing, you'll be unnerved at how much your collegiate has learned. Whether you sent her to Notre Dame or Rosie's College of Bathroom Design, she's become an expert on everything. I'm not referring to math, medieval history, or even tile installation; I mean, the real world. Silly Mom. Silly Dad. All you've done for the past twenty-five years is hold down jobs, run a household, and raise a family. What could you possibly know about how banks work (and why hers keeps returning checks marked "Insufficient Funds"), why the university requires all students to own red convertibles, and why the situation in China, Mexico, Nicaragua, South Africa, and Poland are the direct results of the imperialist American government that your generation brought to power?

Noticeably thinner and poorer, a college student usually spends the Thanksgiving break eating, making phone calls, and washing an enormous amount of clothes that apparently have not experienced detergent and water since they were purchased. Occasionally, ours even conducts a conversation with us.

"How's that computer class going?"

"Okay."

"Do you like your roommate?"

"Yeah."

"Are you having any adjustment problems? Have you been homesick? Are you attending those wild parties we hear about?"

"Huh?"

It's nice to get caught up on all the news.

You might also be surprised to learn that on campus, Coed's most important commitment is watching the daytime dramas (her class schedule is set up so she's free all afternoon.) If it means she must drop psychology or switch her major or even add a fifth year of study to accommodate *Days of Our Lives*, she's willing to make the sacrifice. Such devotion should bring tears to even the most jaded parental eyes.

You probably weep again when you realize that after eighteen years of going to bed at night and getting up in the morning, your freshman's inner clock is on the fritz. You notice this on his first day back when you tiptoe into his bedroom at noon to see if he's still breathing. Should you call the paramedics? you ask Husband fearfully.

"He's probably exhausted from the trip home," your spouse reassures you heartily, ignoring the fact that Frosh has been known to drive fifty miles just to see a good movie. "Let him relax."

By one o'clock, you're holding a mirror in front of Son's lips; by two o'clock, you're vacuuming under his bed; at three, just before you set off some explosives, Sleeping Beauty awakens, spends an hour showering and blow-drying, visits the kitchen to assemble a hearty breakfast of pizza and waffles, which he consumes while watching "Gilligan's Island" reruns with his seven-year-old sister.

At six p.m., as the rest of the family is sitting down to dinner, every eighteen-year-old in the northern hemisphere phones to find out what the evening's plans are. No one seems to know. By eight p.m., when you and Husband leave for a meeting, Frosh is still talking on the phone. "Maybe he'll turn in early tonight," Husband says hopefully.

"Dream on." You sigh. "Unless you mean early in the morning."

Midnight. You're home, the other kids are sleeping, but the mound in Collegiate's bed is a collection of knapsacks and a stale pizza box, not him. You clear a path to the window and gaze at a quiet street. Are they at some major blowout? Cruising down the highway? Attending a holy hour? (Dream on.)

It's 1:30 a.m.—a good time to get some work done on that afghan (or balancing Collegiate's checkbook). Husband is asleep. (How can a man sleep when his child is heaven knows where?) You brew a pot of coffee, sit on the stairs, pace up and down the driveway, and finally decide that if he's not home by 2:30 on the dot, you'll call Mike's mother to find out if the boys are there.

But wait! What if Son isn't at Mike's house? You'll wake

Mike's mother, and she'll end up going through this same scenario. No; better wait another half hour, then call the state police. (Better yet, wake Husband and let him do it.)

At 3:11 a.m., you hear a car pull away and then Son's key in the lock. You resist the impulse to smash a lamp over his head and opt for a come-let-us-reason-together approach. "How come you're home this late?" you shriek. "And don't give me any excuses!"

"I don't have to, Ma." He grins and gives you a gruff bear hug. "I'm in college now. No curfews. You trust me. Remember?"

Could you forget? Dream on.

I believe that we parents must encourage our children to become educated, so they can get into a good college that we cannot afford.

—*Dave Barry*

Has Anyone Seen My . . .

Autumn seems an appropriate time to pause, take stock—and to wonder where my car keys are (to say nothing of the car itself). I never really lose my keys, you understand; I simply misplace them, usually on a daily basis. After a frantic search (and fevered pleas to the angels), they usually turn up in the cookie jar (which hasn't been filled with homemade anything since 2005); by the patio, where I pause in my rounds to pinch a few petunias and speak to the evergreens; or hanging from the trunk lock. When desperate, I borrow my seventeen-year-old's keys, a classy ensemble featuring a key ring teddy bear whose eyes light up whenever one shifts into neutral.

Husband wants to make the keys into a pair of earrings for me so I'll always know where they are. While I appreciate this creative and thoughtful gesture, it doesn't address the ongoing dilemma: why am I always losing things I want to keep, finding things I'd rather lose, and wishing some things would permanently disappear? I know it's a sign of a demented mind, but can it be cured? For example, here's a list of things I once lost:

Our three-year-old. I was in the frozen foods aisle innocently telling a stranger about my hysterectomy. The next thing

I knew, Three had left her sunsuit and diaper in the shopping cart and was cavorting in the bakery department. (She claims she knew exactly where she was during the entire fiasco.) Since then, Husband has accused me of using any excuse to avoid grocery shopping. But honestly, would any sane woman risk it again? Imagine the damage Three could do at the salad bar.

A gerbil of questionable ownership. Apparently, the furry friend was on loan from one of the neighbor kids (no one is owning up to it) and stayed overnight with us one evening when I was otherwise occupied (probably looking for my keys). Warmed by our hospitality, Nip is now rumored to be nesting somewhere in the hall storage closet.

My temper. I lost this first when I heard about Nip, and again when I reviewed the sophomore's school forms. "You didn't tell me you enrolled in advanced lunch, golf, and intermediate study hall," I admonished him. "Isn't that a bit heavy? You know what they say about teen stress. Maybe you should consider a lighter load."

"Funny, Mom," he muttered around a seven-inch-high sandwich. "By the way, here are the health forms, permits, supply and book lists, a requisition for a band percussion instrument, a ballot for the school board election, the Parents' Club membership application, and . . . oh yeah, remember not to fold, spindle, or mutilate."

"The forms or you?"

On the other hand, there are things I wish I could lose, but somehow I can't seem to succeed. Such as

The sixth-grader's collections. It was cute when he kept all his baby teeth and even sweeter when he reserved a shelf for his SpongeBob models and borrowed my file folders for all his school papers. But somehow the pack-rat syndrome took hold, and eventually Son regarded throwing anything away as a matter for confession.

"How about cleaning out some of your drawers?" I asked, looking hopelessly around a bedroom crammed with poster collections, rock collections, and what appeared to be an entire solar system hanging from his ceiling. "Surely you don't need this diagram of the primary colors anymore? Look, if we could throw away these pamphlets, you could actually use this drawer for clothes. People do that, you know."

"But I need that pamphlet collection."

"'The Wonderful World of Squid'? 'Seaweed and You'? Why do you need these?"

"For my aquarium, of course."

"But you don't have . . ."

"Well, I've been meaning to tell you . . ."

Then there are things I hoped I would never find:

Jello in the washing machine. "We were just experimenting, Mom, honest. How could we know it would actually work?"

The utility bills in Husband's gray suit pocket. He was absolutely positively sure he mailed them a week ago Thursday.

Blood anywhere. I have a low courage threshold and have been known to call 911 to report a paper cut. Until one of our offspring enrolled in medical school, I was doomed to hang out windows, shrieking, "Now listen to me, you kids. Stop all that walking around and talking! You're going to get hurt!"

Gray hair. When men go gray, they're viewed as distinguished, not to mention long-suffering, patient, and wise. Grayhaired women, however, are considered ancient. "It's better to be over the hill than under it," Husband attempted to placate me when I inadvertently noticed my first silver threads. But it didn't work. The only solution is to invest in a stylish turban or to dye our hair silver during our teen years so people get used to seeing us that way.

It's true; when raising a family, life always seems upside down. But despite the confusion and chaos, I hope I never lose the awesome realization that God's only a whisper away, everyone's at the table (except Nip), and nothing traumatic happened today. These blessings ought to be enough for any woman.

Caught in the Revolving Door

It happens in most families, so it will probably happen to you. In fact, the return of fully fledged adult children to the barely vacated parental nest presents one of the more intriguing challenges of family life today, and one that parents are accepting with a potent mix of dread, delight, and denial. Here's how it goes:

Step One. Young (presumably upwardly mobile) Adult Offspring informs you that she is leaving home to seek her fame and fortune. You try to refrain from breaking into a tap dance at this news. You muster some false tears and hurry to help her pack before she changes her mind, while babbling about how much the family will miss her.

Step Two. As her car reaches the end of the block, you arrange an impromptu garage sale to liquidate any miscellany left behind, fumigate that upstairs sty, and turn it into the office or sewing room you've always wanted

Step Three. A year later, there's a knock on the door. There stands the traveler, surrounded by seventeen boxes marked "Miscellaneous," three overextended credit cards, and a six-foot boa constrictor named Linguini. She a) is between jobs/roommates/

apartments, b) misses your cooking, or c) says, "You and Dad were right, Mom. I should have finished those last two years of college, and I'm ready now." She's twenty-six.

Step Four. Quietly, you go upstairs, dismantle the sewing room, buy a bed from Goodwill, make her favorite spaghetti for dinner, and don't let any of the younger kids detect your involuntary sobbing except your spouse, who is trying not to let anyone detect his. You, my friend, have just experienced the revolving door syndrome.

In past generations, grown offspring usually stayed home after high school or college or military service, took the first job offer they received, and hung around for a few years, saving for their weddings or perhaps contributing financially to the next child on the ladder. But when they did depart the nest, the flight was usually permanent. Today's young adults, however, do not feel honor-bound to commit the next forty years to one corporation (or one spouse), and the feeling is mutual. Thus, the flotsam of career indecision, failed engagements or marriages, and unbalanced checkbooks is increasingly coming home to roost. According to the census bureau, the number of children still home after the age of twenty-five has increased 200 percent during the last decade. For better or worse, the syndrome has got a lot of us spinning.

We who were just getting used to the non-patter of not-so-little-feet, the custody of our own refrigerator, and the unchallenged right to watch Fox News in detached tranquility must now resume a role we had happily forfeited. And while we love our youngster and want to provide a helping hand, we also sense that our previous parent-child relationship has evolved into something else. We're at a loss: How to define our terms? How to live peacefully with someone who needs independence as well as assistance? Are there any ground rules for this new dilemma from which, it seems, there is no honorable—or affordable—escape? Check the following, culled from the common experience of parents who have survived the revolving door in full command of their senses and their households.

First, it's best to set your terms at the beginning, before your re-rooster has unpacked his poster collection, if possible. Be gracious, be welcoming, and be firm. Yes, of course, he is welcome to share your address, refrigerator, laundry facilities, and parking place, you advise, but *for a limited time*. And a weekly or monthly board payment is expected just as soon as he has landed a job. (Be aware that you can sabotage your own good judgment by not standing firm on this point. Making excuses such as "But she doesn't earn enough" or "He's still paying off his motorcycle" may avoid a tricky subject initially, but they only foster your child's dependence and lack of confidence.)

In our case, our eldest's lease expired, and he came back to live with us for a few months until his wedding, a logical plan with no open-endedness to it. I collected minimal board and used it for wedding expenses. Because we were all aware of the major change just down the road, our time spent together was probably richer too.

Be aware that some kids go in and out of the family abode (hence, the term "revolving") rather than settling in for a longish stay. Typically, Revolvers may only be around until the next good job comes along, and then they are off again. After the third or fourth visit, however, parents are starting to feel like hoteliers, and it's getting harder to fake glad sounds of welcome when the all-too-familiar car pulls into the driveway again. One mom I know went outside with arms wide as her daughter disembarked from her vehicle, and then shouted, "How great to see you! Where will you be staying?"

Daughter's mouth dropped (she had been warned about "the next time,") and she soon found a friend looking for a roommate.

What about house rules? Should curfews be set or activities monitored as in teen days? Perhaps the best wisdom, as one veteran put it, "Rules for adults aren't really necessary if consideration reigns." In other words—does Young Adult phone when she won't be home for dinner, or are you routinely stuck with a six-pound meat loaf for two people? Do your grown-up kids clean up after their midnight food fests, do their laundry, pay their bills on time, pitch in when help is needed, respect you and their younger siblings? If so, they merit *your* respect.

In addition, this expert believes that everyone is entitled to one mistake, so each of her offspring knew that a bed would be waiting for them if they did make a dumb decision out there.

However, if your young adult is falling far short of the maturity mark, it helps to remind yourself that the mortgage says this is *your* house, and the proverbial "Shape Up or Ship Out" option is always available. Or as my friend Ann, a mother of eight, has often put it to one or another, "Tell me what we're doing to make you happy here so we can stop."

Yes, I've heard there are parents so frustrated that they've actually moved in the middle of the night and left their offspring no forwarding address. But that seems a bit drastic. Many seniors have discovered that after the initial reentry shock has waned, they come to truly enjoy this curious transition, especially if there are grandchildren involved. Our grown-up kids can indeed be hazardous to our serenity, but they can also be great new fun, enlivening our midlife passages, bringing exciting ideas and a boost of energy into the house, offering an extra pair of hands now that Mom has probably launched or relaunched her own career. Slowly adult and grown children shift from a parent/child relationship to a friend/friend relationship, and find it a surprisingly pleasant place to be. Slowly, "what do you think?" becomes the standard question rather than "Haven't I told you . . . ?"

Your job is nearly over, but the revolving door has brought an undeniably rich opportunity for new learning together. It will take some changing, some mighty efforts at adjusting—but it's a gift we'd be crazy to refuse.

Human beings are the only creatures on earth that allow their children to come back home.

—*Bill Cosby*

My Thanksgiving Litany

Dear God,

Yes, I know that counting our blessings should be an ongoing habit. But in our hurried preoccupation with everyday living, we often forget just how fortunate we are simply to see, to hear, to be warm and fed and loved. That's why I'm glad there is a Thanksgiving; at least one day each year we're offered a special opportunity to focus our attention on the goodness of life. As a parent, I'm especially grateful for . . .

Diapers, juice bottles, bottom-wiping cloths, paper cups (especially during lemonade-stand season), aluminum roasting pans, and decorated plastic tablecloths. I know, I know. All these goodies can clutter the planet you gave us and unbalance our ecology. But consider the added hours for fun (or arguing) and the nervous breakdowns we avoid.

I'm grateful for the teachers, band directors, Scout leaders, and softball coaches who keep our kids busy—and absent from the home front—for so many hours each year. It takes real dedication (and nerves of cast iron) to work with a segment of the population that never stops hopping, scratching, asking questions, falling off chairs, or telling knock-knock jokes. These people deserve our undying thanks, and perhaps an occasional paid vacation to an intensive care unit.

I'm also grateful to the person who invented the vacuum cleaner and the guy (gal?) who's responsible for sewing extra buttons into the lining of new coats; the designer of the rocking chair, the painless antiseptic (that you can carry in your purse), and the pocket calculator. I appreciate the persons who gave us the ice cube, educational television, and refrigerator magnets. I know I won't meet any of these geniuses until heaven, but their vision has eased my maternal routine considerably. God, if you happen to see any of them, please give them hugs from me.

"What are you doing, Mom?" asks the youngest, stealing a nibble of celery.

"Making the stuffing and counting my blessings."

"Well, don't forget fuzzy teddy bears and nice teachers and the blue jay in our feeder."

Oh, how could I? Praise you, Lord, for you have given us so many things to love. Consider grandparents who give encouragement and support (and even babysitting for fledgling moms and dads). They're especially appreciated for never starting a sentence with "When I was your age . . ." or "If you ask me . . ."

And I can't overlook those other "special people": the supermarket manager who doesn't mind opening a fresh crate of bananas so I can have the pick of the litter; the pediatrician who tells me I'm doing a fine job, though he and I both know I should have reported that strange rash a lot sooner; the school crossing guard at her post through sleet, monsoons, and flying spitballs; and the bridal salon saleswoman who tells me I look lovely in my mother-of-the-groom dress, even though we both know I should have lost that last ten pounds before starting the fittings. I can't overlook our local mechanic who keeps my ancient auto on the road. ("You don't need a new expensive muffler, Mrs. A. We'll just toss on one of these cheap ones and pray a lot.") And who could forget that special neighbor who always says, "I'll have the teen campout/tree-climbing contest/preschool fun fair in my backyard." A true angel.

"What are you doing, Mom?" College Son grabs a handful of raisins.

"Making a pie, hon, and counting my blessings."

"Well, don't forget kids who are old enough to drive to the store for you, big enough to shovel the driveway, and smart enough to get As in science—sometimes."

So true. How often do I dwell on my offspring's good points? They're older now, and we'll be adding our first daughter-in-law to the family very soon. My son showed exceptional wisdom in choosing her to be his wife, and no doubt he learned much of that from me. I guess they were listening to my lectures after all. And God, please let her put up with us . . .

I'm grateful too for the freedom we take so much for granted in this wonderful land, for Fourth of July parades, for letters to the editor voicing vigorous dissent, and for those who gave their lives to make it all possible. I'm grateful for libraries and the awesome amazing Internet, for colleges that happily enroll senior citizens, for fireplaces and popcorn, for quiet conversations and Mozart.

Thank goodness, God, for the joys and failures, challenges and sacrifices that made me more than I ever thought I could be, for laughter and tears and everything in between, for the long-ago dream that has become a Thanksgiving reality.

"What are you doing?" my husband asks, slyly sampling the relish tray.

"Putting the final touches on the feast, and counting my blessings."

"Well, don't forget that the furnace is still working, the kids are upstairs shoveling out their bedrooms, and—I'm so glad you married me."

How could I possibly forget, God? Forever, my blessings are written on my heart.

For each new morning with its light,
For rest and shelter of the night,
For health and food, for love and friends,
For everything Thy goodness sends.

—Ralph Waldo Emerson

Great Expectations

*A**t a* recent party, I was cornered by a couple who had just become grandparents. Well, it was endless: the blow-by-blow account of Daughter-in-Law's labor and delivery (along with Son's magnificent Lamaze-induced assistance). The fuzzy snapshots of a small, red-faced stranger wearing an undershirt. The list of cute/brilliant observations made by older cousins about The New Baby. I was developing a case of terminal yawn by the time Husband rescued me for the journey home.

"Honestly," I complained to the car's interior, "some people make such a big deal out of everything. You'd think no one had ever given birth before."

My better half chuckled. "Sure you're not just a tad jealous?"

"Jealous? Me?" I stopped suddenly as reality intruded. He was right. As the only woman in my circle who has not yet entered the hallowed hierarchy, I've grown defensive, increasingly aware that something is missing in my midlife.

Cuddling a small cooing bundle is such a special experience that one can't be blamed for wanting it to go on and on. But since I'm not willing to try for a spot in the Guinness Book of World Records under Oldest Recorded Pregnancy (I'm having enough trouble with middle-aged spread as it is), responsibility for continuing the family line rightly rests with our offspring.

However, none of them has yet seen fit to make me a Nana. Since no one is married either, this seems the wisest course. But I do admit increasing impatience with their foot-dragging. At a time of life when I should be eating chocolate sandwiches and riding merry-go-rounds with adoring tots, I am instead a bundle of frustration.

Admittedly, the kids are subjected to frequent doses of guilt therapy. "Where did I fail?" and "Why me, God?" are two of my favorites. But nothing changes. Our offspring a) are finishing their educations, b) haven't met the right mate yet, or 3) want to be more financially secure. And while they hide behind these flimsy excuses, years are passing at record speed.

What if, when the moment finally comes, I'm too old to enjoy it? What if I've forgotten all those child-rearing techniques I was too busy to use with my own brood and decided to save for the second time around? I've planned to tread such a perfectly tactful path, beaming as Precious Princess spits up on my husband's boss, refusing to start a sentence with "When I was your age . . ."

And if a three-year-old asks me in a crowded elevator, "Grandma, where did I come from?," this time I'll be prepared.

"Iowa, honey. Have a cookie."

As a recent bumper sticker put it, "Grandchildren are so much fun that we should have had them first." But the timetable isn't up to us anymore.

It's not just for me that I'm hoping. Husband (while somewhat leery of sleeping with a granny) has been primed for the pitter-patter of tiny feet ever since our youngest earned her driver's license. He's longing to love someone who doesn't challenge his every observation, who enjoys hearing him sing "The Teddy Bear's Picnic," someone he can send home when she's naughty . . .

To date, no one of this description has applied for the job.

I'm aware, of course, that the role of "grandmother" has undergone dramatic changes during the past generation or two. No longer is she a white-haired old lady who cleans ovens and grows African violets on her windowsill. Today's Ga-Ga may be single, living in a condo, teaching aerobics, or learning to sky-dive. One of my pals was called out of a corporate boardroom to hear the news that her daughter had delivered; another got word while sunbathing on a cruise ship.

But these Gammies all share a bond—united by their pink or blue brag books, a sudden interest in yarn sales, and a new-found sophistication about disposable diapers, Baby Einstein DVDs, and the latest toy fads. Humbly I listen as they compare notes, rolling their eyes ruefully over babysitting adventures and cracker crumbs in the guest room, debating the relative merits of breast-feeding versus bottle-feeding. How I long to join their secret sorority, but the password is not mine to offer. No one calls me Gram.

And yet, sometimes I sense that this is temporary, that our offspring, so aware of the value of family, will share this gift when the time is right. And I will sing again the old familiar lullabies, feel the old familiar awe that only a parent can know—and, per-haps, only a grandparent can truly appreciate.

In the meantime, there is a lot to do. I'll refinish the rocker, bone up on teething and tetanus, practice flipping a brag book of my own—and wait for the best of all job offers: "Wanted, one grandmother. Responsible only for love."

Grandchildren are God's way of compensating us for growing old.

—Mary H. Waldrip

Christmas Beatitudes

Blessed is December, for Christmas is here.

Blessed are the poor of pocket, for they shall be called parents.

Blessed are the artistic, for they shall wrap everyone's gifts.

Blessed are the peacemakers, for they shall restrain children and pets from knocking over the Christmas tree.

Blessed are they who are heavily laden, for they shall be called shoppers.

Blessed are they who weave paper garlands, produce plays, and wear a confused look, for they shall be called teachers.

Blessed are they who hunger for turkey and trimmings (and happily do the dishes), for they shall be satisfied.

Blessed is the sweater knitted in secret, coins sent to a food bank, dinner for a shut-in, for these shall be called caring.

Blessed are we who, despite the chaos, hold the real Christmas closely in our hearts.

For we shall be called joyful.

The Best
Christmas Present

One of the not-so-sparkly aspects of the Christmas season is the seemingly endless school vacation. This hiatus is supposed to give families a chance for the tender togetherness denied them throughout the rest of the year—and it seems to work on television sitcoms. Characters on our favorite shows are clean, courteous (who wouldn't be in those beautifully decorated houses?), and happy to wait for one another to finish speaking before they insert their own thoughts.

I believe that there are families like that; just because I've never met one doesn't mean that none exist. However, at a neighborhood THWBTN (Thank Heaven We're Back To Normal) coffee gathering last January, I discovered that most parents believe that if educators held school-bond-issue elections during December, they would win overwhelmingly. There's something about being enclosed for almost a month with one's offspring that makes education seem like a real bargain.

For toddlers, the problem is usually the preholiday fever-pitched anticipation (leading wee ones to blow off steam by climbing the Christmas tree) coupled with an after-holiday letdown (leading wee ones to handle boredom by eating candle wax or coloring on Daddy's new shirt.) A preschooler's entire Christmas haul usually depends on several odd-sized batteries available only at a discount store in the next county. With the car still stuck in two feet of driveway snow, such a remedy becomes difficult. In the meantime, tots amuse themselves by tugging on your jeans and whining, running a fever, or eating dirt from the potted plants.

And what is festive about sharing two weeks with a gang of kids who are coming down with cabin fever because of subzero temperatures, who pass the time wrapped in afghans and huddled around the kitchen table, staring out at the blizzard and fretting because the power failure ruined their TV schedule, and who eventually choose arguing as their favorite indoor sport?

"Mom, make him stop bending his elbow!"

"Mom, she's humming again!"

"I'm telling!"

This is the crowd that couldn't wait until the holidays and now spends most of each day following you around to tell you that there's nothing to do-o-o. They can't have friends over because then there would be a whole group with nothing to do-o-o. They can't wash dishes, fumigate their bedrooms, or fill ice cube trays because that's not what kids do-o-o when they're supposed to be on vacation. They can't play Parsimonious (the "in" game that you searched for in seventeen stores) because it turned out to be bor-r-ring after all. These kids can keep busy if you're willing to drive them to a movie in the next county (you could pick up those batteries at the same time), purchase cross-country skis for everyone (this will guarantee about ten minutes of peace before cries of "It's too cold!" or "She's looking at me!" echo across the barren plains), or let them loose in the kitchen with a lot of ice cream, chocolate sauce, and pizza toppings. If none of these solutions appeal to you, ask Spouse to pause in his efforts to fix the washing machine to remind you why being a parent seemed like such a good idea.

The household atmosphere is highly charged anyway due to the receipt of the first semester report cards. Kids who once assured me they were earning straight As must now face the day of reckoning.

"Let's see . . . 'Conduct hinders progress,' 'Does not complete assignments,' 'Does not follow directions' . . ." I peruse the fifth-grader's score sheet.

"I got an 'Excellent' in social studies," he reminds me hopefully.

"That was an attendance grade. Just what do we intend to do about this situation, pal?"

He sighs. "I'd better quit my paper route and stop helping around the house. I need more time to study."

"How about quitting TV-watching and hanging around the candy store after school?" I suggest sweetly.

"Mom! I gotta have *some* fun! 'All work and no play . . .'"

"Is going to get you off probation next semester. Got it?"

"Yep."

Then, of course, there is the resident adolescent. This is the youngster you actually miss because he is not around that often anymore, the one you fondly assume will at last be willing and eager to communicate with you on an adult level. Unfortunately this is also the person who has just finished a semester of psychology.

You: Good morning, honey. How was work last night?

Son: What work?

You: Your job. Weren't you slinging burgers last night at Hamburger Heaven?

Son: Why do you ask?

You: Why? Because I'm interested. I was wondering if any of your friends are working there, how they're enjoying vacation . . .

Son: You want me to find out for you?

You: No! I just wanted to know how work went last night, that's all.

Son: Have we even established that I worked last night, Mom? And why are you so suspicious? Does it have something to do with your past? Or are you going through another midlife crisis? Do you want to talk about it?

You: Answer the phone, will you?

The phone. On days when no power failures occur, it can be your lifeline to other cabin-fevered parents. But you have to gain custody of the device first, and this can be tricky in a household full of kids spending vacation telling other kids how bor-r-ring vacation is. The best way is to schedule a calling hour for yourself—sometime after vacuuming up the crushed holly but before readdressing the Christmas cards (returned on December 26th because someone forget to attach postage.)

Yes, the days seem endless, and wouldn't it make more sense to add them onto the end of summer when students are required to begin classes while the pavement is still buckling? Or . . . we could leave the Christmas holiday break the same length but, by law, all cold-climate residents would be required to take their families to Florida for the duration. Travel expenses to be covered by Congress.

Indeed, long, frigid vacations are not my idea of bliss. And yet, in our enforced midwinter togetherness, perhaps our family learns some valuable lessons we might miss in a more pleasant setting. We adjust to one another's moods and argue until the restlessness is assuaged. We decide that it might be fun to be friends again. We cope, compensate, recreate, discover, laugh, share batteries, cry, and generally *live*, and in doing so, we become aware of the faithfulness of family, the only love and acceptance that continues no matter what.

It may not be the most noticeable gift under the tree, but it's no doubt the best.

To us, family means putting your arms around each other and being there.

—*Barbara Bush*

Postscript

In case you were wondering, it was a great wedding. I had spent almost an entire book wondering about how everything would work out, but it did. Not only did our future daughter-in-law decide to take the gamble and join our family, the videos show her smiling all day. (Could she have faked that? *Would* she have faked that?)

The couple's siblings were all attendants (girls wearing red), and both bride and groom came down the aisle on the arms of both of their parents, a nice gesture. I wore a light pink dress, which didn't actually pass for beige, but it was close. (I was not able to keep my mouth shut, but you knew that, didn't you?) Given that the happy couple had met at a prayer group, the music ministry decided to play for the wedding mass, and play they did! (How many wedding ceremonies have you attended where the congregation was clapping along with the final song?) The priest was no stranger to praise and worship music either, and I decided not to wonder what guests from other faiths were thinking about our exuberant ceremony . . .

The reception was great fun. Traditional, of course, with bouquet- and garter-tossing, and a lovely first dance. Groom and Third Son entertained party-goers with one of their impromptu comedy dialogues, this one between Harry Carey and Steve Stone of Chicago Cubs fame. The photographer laughed so hard that he lost hold of his equipment. Fourth Son joined in with an Andy Rooney routine, but at this point we called a halt due to a second broken camera.

I'd had a little talk with Future Daughter-in-Law before the big day. I'd explained to her that ours was a family of extroverts (no, she was not surprised). "We love a good debate," I told her, "and we give advice without waiting to be asked. This means that despite our intentions, we will probably all have comments about anything you say or do for the rest of your life . . ." Daughter-in-Law was looking slightly alarmed, so I hurried on.

". . . So the way to get through this is simply to smile sweetly as we babble, and then do exactly as you please," I finished. "No one will ever ask you how it all turned out—we will have moved on to new arguments. Get it?" She did, and to this day she still likes us (or seems to), and the feeling is definitely mutual.

I guess she was right that day so long ago, when she pointed out that God had had His hand on us since the beginning of time. It's hard to understand these things as we go through them, but in hindsight, a lot of it makes sense. I can see now how well we have been guided by our guardian angels, and how they have drawn us all closer to God and His kingdom through the years. And I hope they stick around for the next chapter in our lives . . .

Grandchildren.

I'm not going to vacuum until Sears makes one you can ride on.

—Roseanne Barr

About the Author

*J*oan Wester Anderson began her writing career in 1973 with a series of family humor articles for local newspapers and Catholic publications. She was a monthly columnist for two national magazines during the 1980s. She has published more than one thousand articles and short stories in a variety of publications, including *Woman's Day, Modern Bride, Virtue, Reader's Digest,* and the *New York Times Syndicate.*

Her book *Where Angels Walk, True Stories of Heavenly Visitors* was on the *New York Times* bestseller list for over a year, has sold almost two million copies, and has been translated into fourteen languages. *Where Miracles Happen* and *An Angel to Watch*

Over Me were written in response to suggestions from readers and were followed in rapid succession by three more in the series. *Forever Young*, the life story of actress Loretta Young, was published in November 2000. The actress had read the angel series and requested Anderson as her biographer. The two became close friends. *In the Arms of Angels* covers angelic activity primarily during the past decade, including stories of hope from the 9/11 and Columbine School tragedies. Her most recent books, *Guardian Angels*, *Angels and Wonders*, and *Angelic Tales*, focus on amazing and tender stories of God's answers to prayers.

Anderson has appeared on several national television programs, including *Good Morning America*, *Oprah*, *20/20*, *NBC Nightly News with Tom Brokaw*, and *Mother Angelica Live*. She was featured in such documentaries as "Angels—Beyond the Light" (NBC), "Angel Stories," "Stories of Miracles" (The Learning Channel), and many videos. She was a story consultant for the television series *It's a Miracle*. She lectures in cities across the country and has been interviewed on hundreds of radio talk shows.

Anderson is a Catholic and a member of St. Edna's Parish in Arlington Heights, Illinois. She graduated from Northeastern Illinois University in Chicago, is a member of the American Society of Journalists and Authors, and is a former adjunct professor at Harper Community College in Palatine, Illinois. She and her husband live in suburban Chicago and have five grown children and five grandchildren.